Cabaret

Forms of Drama

Forms of Drama meets the need for accessible, mid-length volumes that offer undergraduate readers authoritative guides to the distinct forms of global drama. From classical Greek tragedy to Chinese pear garden theatre, cabaret to *kathakali*, the series equips readers with models and methodologies for analysing a wide range of performance practices and engaging with these as 'craft'.

SERIES EDITOR: SIMON SHEPHERD

Cabaret
978-1-3501-4025-7
William Grange

Pageant
978-1-3501-4451-4
Joan FitzPatrick Dean

Satire
978-1-3501-4007-3
Joel Schechter

Tragicomedy
978-1-3501-4430-9
Brean Hammond

Cabaret

William Grange

methuen | drama

LONDON • NEW YORK • OXFORD • NEW DELHI • SYDNEY

METHUEN DRAMA
Bloomsbury Publishing Plc
50 Bedford Square, London, WC1B 3DP, UK
1385 Broadway, New York, NY 10018, USA
29 Earlsfort Terrace, Dublin 2, Ireland

BLOOMSBURY, METHUEN DRAMA and the Methuen Drama logo are
trademarks of Bloomsbury Publishing Plc

First published in Great Britain 2021

Series design by Charlotte Daniels

A catalogue record for this book is available from the British Library.

Library of Congress Control Number: 2021938163

ISBN:	HB:	978-1-3501-4026-4
	PB:	978-1-3501-4025-7
	ePDF:	978-1-3501-4028-8
	eBook:	978-1-3501-4027-1

Series: Forms of Drama

Typeset by Integra Software Services Pvt Ltd
Printed and bound in Great Britain

To find out more about our authors and books visit www.bloomsbury.com
and sign up for our newsletters.

CONTENTS

LIST OF
ILLUSTRATIONS

SERIES PREFACE

The scope of this series is scripted aesthetic activity that works by means of personation.

Scripting is done in a wide variety of ways. It may, most obviously, be the more or less detailed written text familiar in the stage play of the Western tradition, which not only provides lines to be spoken but directions for speaking them. Or it may be a set of instructions, a structure or scenario, on the basis of which performers improvise, drawing, as they do so, on an already learnt repertoire of routines and responses. Or there may be nothing written, just sets of rules, arrangements, and even speeches orally handed down over time. The effectiveness of such unwritten scripting can be seen in the behaviour of audiences, who, without reading a script, have learnt how to conduct themselves appropriately at the different activities they attend. For one of the key things that unwritten script specifies and assumes is the relationship between the various groups of participants, including the separation, or not, between doers and watchers.

What is scripted is specifically an aesthetic activity. That specification distinguishes drama from non-aesthetic activity using personation. Following the work of Erving Goffman in the mid-1950s, especially his book *The Presentation of Self in Everyday Life*, the social sciences have made us richly aware of the various ways in which human interactions are performed. Going shopping, for example, is a performance in that we present a version of ourselves in each encounter we make. We may indeed have changed our clothes before setting out. This, though, is a social performance.

The distinction between social performance and aesthetic activity is not clear-cut. The two sorts of practice overlap and mingle with one another. An activity may be more or less aesthetic, but the crucial distinguishing feature is the status of the aesthetic element. Going shopping may contain an aesthetic element – decisions about clothes and shoes to wear – but its purpose is not deliberately to make an aesthetic activity or to mark itself as different from everyday social life. The aesthetic element is not regarded as a general requirement. By contrast a court-room trial may be seen as a social performance, in that it has an important social function, but it is at the same time extensively scripted, with prepared speeches, costumes, and choreography. This scripted aesthetic element assists the social function in that it conveys a sense of more than everyday importance and authority to proceedings which can have life-changing impact. Unlike the activity of going shopping, the aesthetic element here is not optional. Derived from tradition it is a required component that gives the specific identity to the activity.

It is defined as an activity in that, in a way different from a painting of Rembrandt's mother or a statue of Ramesses II, something is made to happen over time. And, unlike a symphony concert or firework display, that activity works by means of personation. Such personation may be done by imitating and interpreting – 'inhabiting' – other human beings, fictional or historical, and it may use the bodies of human performers or puppets. But it may also be done by a performer who produces a version of their own self, such as a stand-up comedian or court official on duty, or by a performer who, through doing the event, acquires a self with special status as with the *hijras* securing their sacredness by doing the ritual practice of *badhai*.

Some people prefer to call many of these sorts of scripted aesthetic events not drama but cultural performance. But there are problems with this. First, such labelling tends to keep in place an old-fashioned idea of Western scholarship that drama, with its origins in ancient Greece, is a specifically European 'high' art. Everything outside it is then potentially, and damagingly, consigned to a domain which may be neither 'art' nor 'high'. Instead the European stage play and its like can best be regarded as a subset of the general category, distinct from the rest in that two groups of people come together in order specifically to present and watch a story being acted out by imitating other persons and settings. Thus, the performance of a stage play in this tradition consists of two levels of activity using personation: the interaction of audience and performers and the interaction between characters in a fictional story.

The second problem with the category of cultural performance is that it downplays the significance and persistence of script, in all its varieties. With its roots in the traditional behaviours and beliefs of a society script gives specific instructions for the form – the materials, the structure, and sequence – of the aesthetic activity, the drama. So too, as we have noted, script defines the relationships between those who are present in different capacities at the event.

It is only by attending to what is scripted, to the form of the drama, that we can best analyse its functions and pleasures. At its most simple analysis of form enables us to distinguish between different sorts of aesthetic activity. The masks used in *kathakali* look different from those used in *commedia dell'arte*. They are made of different materials, designs, and colours. The roots of those differences lie in their separate cultural traditions and systems of living. For similar reasons the puppets of *karagoz* and *wayang* differ. But perhaps more importantly the attention to form provides a basis for exploring the operation and effects of a particular work. Those who regularly participate in and watch drama, of whatever sort, learn to recognize and remember the forms of what they see and hear. When one drama has family resemblances to another, in its organization and use of materials, structure, and sequences, those who attend it develop expectations as to how it will – or indeed should – operate. It then becomes possible to specify how a particular work subverts, challenges, or enhances these expectations.

Expectation doesn't only govern response to individual works, however. It can shape, indeed has shaped, assumptions about which dramas are worth studying. It is well established

that Asia has ancient and rich dramatic traditions, from the
Indian sub-continent to Japan, as does Europe, and these are
studied with enthusiasm. But there is much less widespread
activity, at least in Western universities, in relation to the
traditions of, say, Africa, Latin America, and the Middle
East. Second, even within the recognized traditions, there are
assumptions that some dramas are more 'artistic', or indeed
more 'serious', 'higher' even, than others. Thus, it may be
assumed that *noh* or classical tragedy will require the sort of
close attention to craft which is not necessary for mumming
or *badhai*.

Both sets of assumptions here keep in place a system which
allocates value. This series aims to counteract a discriminatory
value system by ranging as widely as possible across world
practices and by giving the same sort of attention to all the
forms it features. Thus book-length studies of forms such
as *al-halqa*, *hana keaka*, and *ta'zieh* will appear in English
for perhaps the first time. Those studies, just like those of
kathakali, tragicomedy, and the rest, will adopt the same basic
approach. That approach consists of an historical overview of
the development of a form combined with, indeed anchored
in, detailed analysis of examples and case studies. One of the
benefits of properly detailed analysis is that it can reveal the
construction which gives a work the appearance of being
serious, artistic, and indeed 'high'.

What does that work of construction is script. This series
is grounded in the idea that all forms of drama have script
of some kind and that an understanding of drama, of any
sort, has to include analysis of that script. In taking this
approach, books in this series again challenge an assumption
which has in recent times governed the study of drama.
Deriving from the supposed, but artificial, distinction between
cultural performance and drama, many accounts of cultural
performance ignore its scriptedness and assume that the proper
way of studying it is simply to describe how its practitioners
behave and what they make. This is useful enough, but to leave
it at that is to produce something that looks like a form of

lesser anthropology. The description of behaviors is only the
first step in that it establishes what the script is. The next step is
to analyse how the script and form work and how they create
effect.

But it goes further than this. The close-up analyses of
materials, structures, and sequences – of scripted forms – show
how they emerge from and connect deeply back into the modes
of life and belief to which they are necessary. They tell us in
short why, in any culture, the drama needs to be done. Thus by
adopting the extended model of drama, and by approaching
all dramas in the same way, the books in this series aim to
tell us why, in all societies, the activities of scripted aesthetic
personation – dramas – keep happening, and need to keep
happening.

I am grateful, as always, to Mick Wallis for helping me to think
through these issues. Any clumsiness or stupidity is entirely my
own.

                                        Simon Shepherd

ACKNOWLEDGMENTS

I would like to thank Matthias Thiel, the director of the German Cabaret Archive in Mainz, for his valuable help and suggestions.

William Grange

Introduction

There is general agreement among scholars and cultural historians that Montmartre, in the eighteenth arrondissement of Paris, was the birthplace of modern cabaret, a particular manifestation of live performance. The wider use of the term "cabaret" began there in the mid-1880s. The venues where it took place were cramped, while containing a raised stage and a congested seating space. Customers congregated in close proximity to one another, and the intimacy of the experience was important. Tight spaces and intimate surroundings promoted eye-to-eye contact between performers and spectators, a corollary of the impulse toward "small is beautiful" among reformers like John Ruskin (1819–1900). The word from which "cabaret" descended also described a small space, namely *chambrette*, or "little room." It appears in some French texts by the thirteenth century, and some scholars believe its earliest cognate may have been common in the Picard language, a French patois spoken in the northernmost parts of what is today northern France and Belgium. By the mid-seventeenth century, "cabaret" was in fairly frequent circulation, used to distinguish an eatery from a tavern. Cabarets differed from taverns in Paris because they also served food on a plate, and some cabarets even covered their tables with a heavy linen cloth. Cabarets were not specifically

associated with entertainment, though musicians and singers
sometimes performed in them.

The practice of cabaret subsequent to its birth in
Montmartre, which many of its admirers, adherents, and even
its practitioners described as an "epidemic" or "contagion,"
adapted itself to national norms of legal, financial, and social
consequence. Performers in Berlin, Munich, Vienna, Prague,
Budapest, Krakow, and elsewhere, however, maintained
certain characteristics that were originally present. What
began as a gathering of poets and balladeers mutated in ways
that expanded cabaret's musical range, adding attributes such
as dance, transvestitism, topical commentary, and a master of
ceremonies. Film has succeeded in expanding public perception
of cabaret, though often as a somewhat debauched emblem
of social decline or sexual licentiousness. Most readers will
have seen or become familiar with *The Blue Angel* (1930) and
Cabaret (1972), two films that feature cabaret performances
prominently, and in which the lead female characters are
agents of degeneracy. There are dozens of other films in which
cabaret scenes take place and conspicuously feature moral
indiscretion; they include (among many others) *Les Dames
du Bois de Boulogne* (1945), *Lola* (1961), *The Serpent's Egg*
(1977), *Just a Gigolo* (1979), *Victor Victoria* (1982), and
the recent television series *Babylon Berlin* (2017). Cabaret's
general history, however, does not reflect an abundance of
impropriety, despite the suspicions of many viewers who have
attended such films. Its roots lie in a mid-nineteenth-century
bohemianism that poets, fiction writers, law enforcement
officials, several critics, historians, and observers considered
noteworthy.

Jürgen Henningsen, himself a cabaret performer, has
written that cabaret's history reveals a performance art
based on "an acquired set of coherencies" (*erworbene
Wissenszusammenhang*) that is sensitive to contemporary
trends, manias, fads, and affectations. Yet cabaret remains
curiously reluctant to "cut itself off from the umbilical cord
of its history" (1967: 11). In other words, cabaret contains

within it a pre-Montmartrian tradition of what Karl Vossler termed "universal entertainers": buffoons, acrobats, tumblers, minstrels, mummers, maskers, contortionists, jokesters, and other varieties of popular entertainers (1898: 102). Among them, the troubadours in medieval Europe enjoyed a higher status than did most, because the troubadour possessed intellectual qualities. In his songs, the troubadour displayed a mastery of both song and poetry, and he may well have been among the first *Vortragskünstler* (roughly translated as "stand-up comedian"). The troubadour, like a stand-up comedian, had to keep his material up-to-date if he wanted to maintain a connection with his audience. Why? Because cabaret's impact "depends on the collectively acquired set of coherencies among the audience. Cabaret's effectiveness is not independent of audience expectations—and those expectations change quite rapidly" (Henningsen 1967: 12).

Audience membership at a cabaret performance is not always comfortable. Aristide Bruant often insulted his paying audiences, much to their amusement. Volker Ludwig of the Reichskabarett in Berlin from 1965 to 1971 described his experience:

> We accused former Nazi professors of murder and they applauded. We told industrialists they were nothing but exploiters, workers of total corruption, and they all cheered in unison. We accused newspapers of dumbing down their reviews because their readers were basically illiterate, and the newspaper critics loved us. We hurled insults at everybody, we pointed fingers at them and cursed them for their hypocrisy, cowardice, and their thuggery. Everybody thought we were sensational.
>
> (Ludwig 1966: 7)

Cabaret avoids the pathetic or melodramatic. Rarely does any cabaret performer sing an aria or shed tears over lost money. A lost wallet or a lack of money, however, is often a gag in cabaret routines. Purpose almost always surmounts means; the purpose is usually laughter, and the means is often a gag. The gag may have pathetic or melodramatic contours, but there are some borders nobody should cross. Borders in cabaret are defined by the established place and time in which a sketch operates. As opposed to the actor, the cabaret performer cannot jump out of the concrete situation of the space he has created (Henningsen 1967: 18). With Bertolt Brecht, one can say that the cabaret artist "shows" himself onstage, but he is not that self. But in cabaret, the performer assumes a kind of personality type. The role, such as it is, is "merely insinuated," much like a cap that sits atop one's head insinuated that the head belongs to a taxi driver. Such insinuations are more effective than entire costumes. The cabaret performer should therefore avoid "suffering" anything or becoming a martyr. If he curses something, he should laugh while doing so. "Propriety" or "decorum" is foreign to cabaret. Anything that resembles the bromides heard in the halls of government, the church, or in the school classroom is taboo unless the performer is satirizing those bromides as platitudes. No cabaret performer should make the mistake of wanting to be taken seriously.

The "play of an acquired set of coherencies" is particularly evident as a "linguistically developed experience" (*eine sprachlich erschlossene Erfahrung*) (Henningsen 1967: 24). Within this experience is the knowledge that water is wet everywhere, that the sun rises in the east and sets in the west. That knowledge comprises an aggregate of "not yet" forgotten facts, assumptions, and information. But cabaret becomes successful only as far as the audience's perception of assumptions can take them. Actual fact is subordinate to the subjective response to the fact. A good metaphor for cabaret is a house of cards. The house is not stable and it easily collapses in on itself, creating a minor comic effect. Audience response depends on the performer's relationship to the house of cards. He can make it collapse, for example, by pulling a card out (a technique Henningsen calls "debunking"). He can also cause it to collapse if he overloads one side of the house with one too many cards, a technique he calls "caricature."

He can also replace one card with another, called "travesty," or using "cheaper" cards to replace the more expensive ones, called "parody." Travesty is the conventional retention of content but in an unconventional form, as when Bugs Bunny sings an aria from *The Barber of Seville.* Parody, on the other hand, is retaining the conventional form but filling it with unconventional content (Henningsen 1967: 37). A truly vulgar (and very popular) example is a cabaret performer singing Figaro's recitative "Figaro hier, Figaro dort" (Figaro here, Figaro there) to the lyric "Ficke mal hier, ficke mal dort" (fuck around here, fuck around there). Comic collisions are an important part of cabaret humor, occasioned by travesty and grotesquerie. Georg Kriesler's song "Das Mädchen mit den drei blauen Augen" (The Girl with the Three Blue Eyes) is a good example of how the grotesque can feed travesty. The song sounded folksy and resembled the form of a love ballad, but something was lurking behind it: if an Aryan girl had blue eyes, then a three-eyed girl was even more Aryan. Another formal comic device favored in cabaret is what Henningsen calls the "omission gimmick." For example, two young women are discussing men: one tells her friend, "I stopped going out with my boyfriend. He knows too many dirty songs." "Oh yeah?" asks her friend. "Does he sing them to you?" "No," comes the reply. "He plays them on the flute."

The crucial factor in the effectiveness of such material is the aforementioned concept of "small," which has compelling significance in cabaret. The word applies to space in which cabaret performances take place, the number of individuals in the cast of performers, the budgets upon which cabarets operate, and the reach of cabaret's effectiveness. It ideally refers to the intellectual compactness of the program: various subjects proceed as performed sketches rapidly follow each other from one to the next, often with comments in between them from a master of ceremonies. No intellectual depths are plumbed, no "intimacy" is implied (in the sense of Strindberg's attempt at the turn of the century "to concentrate on a subject or idea intensely") (Sprengel 1998: 450).

The space in which cabaret takes place is confining, as noted above. Its purpose is to allow the spectator to experience the nuances of performance, the direct care with which the performer shares his or her art with the viewer, and in certain moments to experience the sensation that the performer and viewer have exchanged roles (Bayerdörfer 1978: 308). In the closed space of cabaret certain social customs and expectations are suspended, as the audience member seeks distraction from everyday life and a release from expectations of "normal" behavior. The desire for entertainment is satisfied, the craving for human contact is fulfilled, and the sense of "togetherness" is realized. The togetherness of cabaret does not result from artistry per se, however. The sense of "community" in cabaret is something imparted throughout the space, beginning with the satisfaction of physical and intellectual demands, though such demands are altogether different from one another.

Spending an evening at a cabaret performance erases differences among people and temporarily dissolves the perception of disparities among them. The small and limited space assures such dissolution, temporary though it may be: the "stage" is miniscule, usually no more than a platform of some kind. Customers sit at small tables, where they can drink, smoke, and eat during the show. The stage, such as it is, offers no barriers and does not support a sense of separation among customers and performers. There is a general atmosphere of freedom, even of equanimity within the space. And this atmosphere has nothing to do with theater's antecedents of spiritual uplift. At the time of cabaret's emergence as a genre, there were demands among some intellectual critics that live performance should examine social problems, as if those problems were amenable to some kind of playful analysis. Cabaret rejects such analyses, though it considers them at times the targets of its orientation. When cabaret takes social or political questions into consideration, it often does so in the form of musical verse or in couplets that feature clever rhyme schemes. It attempts to capture the customer's attention with sound and sight, not with earnestness of thought. If it does consider political questions, it usually does so with derision and mockery. Cabaret is a child of the "impudent muse," and that child had several mothers: Yvette Guilbert, Marya Delvard, Claire Waldoff, Emmy Hennings, Rosa Valetti, and Trude Hesterberg among the most notable, as we shall see.

Within the unceremonious atmosphere of cabaret, the tradition of respectful veneration toward the artist disappears, as does the appreciative gratitude of the artist to the audience. Performers insult customers, and customers gleefully respond. The tradition of mutual dependency between performers and customers, however, temporarily recedes in cabaret. Hanns Heinz Ewers described this phenomenon as something which many found irresistible: an opportunity to experience the artist face to face, in a way that was incomparable in any other art form. "It was the proximity to artists in their element, creating art before your very eyes and ears," he said. Cabaret puts the customer in the place where the artists create their work, even as they create it. Cabaret was not something that artists formulated somewhere else and then wore a tuxedo to present it. "Imagine Bruant in a tuxedo—it would have been ridiculous!" In cabaret, the sense of authenticity is undeniable. It is unpolished. It holds nothing back (1904: 39).

The term "small" is relative, because not all German cabaret took place in small spaces. There were 650 seats in the first German cabaret, the *Überbrettl* of Wolzogen, and about 1,000 seats in the first *Schall und Rauch* (Noise and Smoke). The term "small" infers "closeness" or "tight" or "closely packed," alluding to "physical proximity." Valeska Hirsch Lindtberg, who played piano for Erika Mann at the Zurich *Pfeffermühle* (Pepper Grinder), said that the tables and chairs at the Golden Stag Hotel in Zurich were packed together so closely that when the place was sold out, nobody could move from their seats. Lindtberg claimed that customers sat so close to her that they could easily have played four-handed on the piano's keyboard. The tiny stage offered no traditional exits or entrances, except for a ladder that descended from an upstairs dressing room down onto the stage. Nobody complained about such close quarters, but it was often uncomfortable.

Cabaret thrives on the directness of performance and its rehearsed spontaneity, made possible through the reciprocal interaction of performers and audience. This interaction arises from the rapid transition between sketches, from the interplay of language in the form of recited or sung composition, accompanied by body language (mimicry, gesture, vocalization, or movement) and the apprehension of various arts, for example, poetry, music, dance, scenic design, architecture, painting, and set decoration. To cabaret belongs likewise the sensual pleasures of food and drink, along with the intellectual pleasures of conversation and sociable interaction while the performance is taking place. But above all cabaret thrives on the directness and the irrevocability of the occasion. In other words, one can make the claim that cabaret *happens* or takes place, but it exists only in the moment of performance. Therein lies its eventful character: cabaret as a whole is by its very nature transitory and ephemeral, even when it has been extensively rehearsed. Cabaret lives as a genre only in the here and now of the performance.

As a composite whole, cabaret mandates its own set of aesthetic principles, which have nothing to do with the aesthetics of sketches, songs, dances, or stand-up comedy contained within it. A reconstruction of the whole is merely a conjectural undertaking, and it can be accomplished only in writing, which rarely aligns with reality—at least not with historical reality. "You had to have been there," one must assume. "Cabaret should look as if it had been put together by dilettantes, and it must also emerge as if it had just happened at that particular moment. The routines must look only barely accomplished, and the ensemble should appear slightly under-rehearsed, and the viewer must have a vague sense of watching from the outside as the performers enjoy themselves" (Friedell 1985: 218).

The chapters which follow in this volume concentrate on performers, composers, lyricists, economic developments, technologies, and political events which provided the most significant impetus to cabaret's emergence and development.

There are thus a significant number of influences which remain noteworthy by virtue of their absence. The predominant artistic presence, however, of Aristide Bruant, Yvette Guilbert, Ernst von Wolzogen, Marya Delvard, Rudolf Nelson, Claire Waldoff, Frank Wedekind, Werner Finck, Trude Hesterberg, Endre Nagy, Kathi Kobus, Karel Hašler, Emmy Hennings, Tadeusz Boy-Zelenski, Blandine Ebinger, and Friedrich Hollaender may overshadow at times others whose contributions remain compelling. Yet others may emerge from the shadows of history and take their place in the cabaret spotlight; their number must certainly include Joachim Albert von Hohenzollern, Franz Wärndorfer, Jiri Cerveny, Rodolphe Salis, Rosa Valetti, Julius Bierbaum, and Egon Friedell. The latter group of individuals often provided financial or organizational talent that helped the former group to create and, for brief periods of time, survive in a marketplace fraught with hazards.

Those hazards include major wars, financial catastrophes, technological disruptions, legal obstructions, political cataclysms, and vast social upheavals. Cabaret had its beginnings, for example, in class conflict. Other advocates of cabaret believed that cabaret's first "duty" was to battle widespread philistinism and prudery. The emphasis on the "small stage" credo of the cabaret environment had its roots in the British "arts and crafts movement" of the mid-nineteenth-century Great Britain—yet, cabaret made little headway in Britain. Many of the stances taken among cabaret's performers and supporters were anti-militarist, though several artists served with distinction in military units of their various countries. Cabaret began as an extrapolation on live performance at café-concerts, follies-style diversions, and variety shows—yet, the publication of cabaret music, sketches, and the sale of its musical recordings helped to actuate a public perception of cabaret as mass entertainment.

About half of this volume's inquiries are devoted to German-language cabaret, largely because German cabaret culture flourished and intensified after the initial cabaret precedent in France. German cabaret at first differed markedly from the French, but it ironically tended to adhere more closely to French antecedents as it matured. That adherence was due in part to Marc Henry, a French cabaret performer who helped establish cabaret in Munich and later in Vienna. The cabaret in Berlin is most well-known; it produced some of the most prodigious cabaret talents to emerge anywhere, and their influence remained significant for decades after the "Golden Age" of Berlin cabaret in the 1920s.

German-language cabaret also benefits from the presence of three major archives, in which materials documenting cabaret activities are housed and where scholars and historians from around the world conduct primary research. The German Cabaret Archive in Mainz began in 1961 as the private collection of scholar Reinhard Hippen (1942–2010). In 1989 the City of Mainz assumed responsibility for the Archive, with Klaus Budzinski (1921–2016) as its director. Together Budzinski and Hippen produced the *Metzler-Kabarett-Lexikon* in 1996. The Swiss Cabaret Archive in Thun opened in 2000, and the Austrian Cabaret Archive is located in Graz, which opened in 2001. The German cabaret also remains the most well-organized of any. The City of Mainz and its Cabaret Archive has awarded its *Kleinkunstpreis* every year since 1972. Sometimes those prizes go to individuals for excellence over a long career (such as the one awarded to Gert Fröbe[1] in 1976), and sometimes to ensembles whose work the Archive has found exemplary. In 1982, the Arbeitsgemeinschaft für Unterhaltung deutschsprachiger Sender (Association of Entertainers in German Broadcasting) began to award it "Salzburg Bull"[2] for outstanding cabaret-style work in German on television and radio.

1

Beginnings in France

Montmartre

Among the most notable of seventeenth-century Parisian cabarets during the reign of Louis XIII were The Fox, The Three Golden Bridges, and The Cross of Lorraine. The most "literary" (i.e., where Parisians met to argue about literature) of them all was thought to be a place called The Pine Cone. During the reign of Louis XIV, the favorite hangout of Moliére and Racine (when they were still on speaking terms) was a cabaret called the White Sheep. The cabaret favored by courtiers at the court of Louis XIV was *La Boisselière*, near the Tuileries Palace. This cabaret had no name, but mistress of the house was Mme. Boisselière. Dinner at her place cost five times that of an ordinary cabaret in Paris (*Household Words* 1857: 115). Food was important at cabarets, almost as important as arguing about poetry, gossiping about sex and politics at court, or drinking affordable wine.

By the mid-nineteenth century in Paris the term "cabaret" had fallen out of everyday use, though there certainly remained several venues where customers met to discuss literature, politics, or art. Such informal gatherings in public houses with alcoholic beverages on offer were abundant in

Parisian neighborhoods. In some of those public houses one
could hear poets, essayists, scribes, translators, copyists, and
others with literary ambitions read their efforts aloud to what
they hoped would be a sympathetic audience. The audiences
were an elite company, many being members of literary
clubs that had emerged in the 1850s. All of the presenters
were desirous of finding a market for their endeavors. By the
end of the 1870s, proprietors of public houses, wine bars,
taverns, hostelries, and similar establishments discovered the
unexpected profitability of readings open to the public. What
made the arrangement doubly promising for the proprietor
was the readiness of writers and balladmongers to present
their work free of charge even while audience members were
willing to pay an admission fee.

There were of course other forces at work in the process
of conceiving the child that grew up to become the modern
cabaret. One of the forces was legislative, which resulted
in the so-called *embourgoisement* of public performance
in 1864. A decree of the Emperor's Household in that year
liberalized ownership of theaters in Paris (a similar law went
into effect in Berlin five years later), and in 1867 the French
government's head of theater administration ruled that
"café-concerts" were henceforth permitted to use costumes
and other articles of scenic investiture. Such use was
previously restricted to opera and spoken drama, and the
measure broadened the popularity of the "café-concerts." By
1872 there were more than 150 such venues in Paris. Café-
concerts were what one might best describe as a middlebrow
musical extravaganza, though many were extremely modest;
most had a mini-stage, with no special dramaturgy. Singers
alternated and mostly performed their own songs and lyrics.
Some café-concerts, however, were elaborate and attracted
substantial audience numbers. All featured singers and
musical accompaniment, and after the legislative relaxation
of 1867 they began to resemble what some observers have
called music halls.

The Bohemians

The second major influence on the emergence of modern cabaret was the socio-cultural structure of Paris. In the years following the collapse of the Second Empire during the brief Franco-Prussian War (1870–1), the separated hill-top suburb of Montmartre retained its reputation as a refuge not only for certain criminal elements, but also for certain kinds of non-conformists known as "bohemians." The etymology of *bohême* or *bohêmien* to signify immigrant beggars in the fifteenth century from Eastern Europe (sometimes called *gitane*, or "gypsies") is fairly well acknowledged. The term first gained circulation in Paris during 1840, when Honore de Balzac published a novel titled *Un prince de la bohème* (A Prince of Bohemia). Its use as a signifier of non-conformity or even to equate it with the repudiation of bourgeois behavioral norms is inexact. That usage probably emerged during the early stages of European industrialization, when middle-class viewpoints came to dominate much of European print media. In those years the French police used the term to identify individuals living in low-rent, crime-ridden Parisian neighborhoods. The provenance of the term's use to describe avant-garde artists, literary pretenders, entertainers of various stripes, anarchists, and other semi-disreputable characters is more easily determined, especially as the term became international.

In 1845, a French writer named Henri Murger (1822–61) began publishing stories he called *Scènes de la vie de bohème* (Scenes from Bohemian Life) in a literary journal called *Le Corsaire Satan* (The Satanic Corsair). Mergur belonged to a loosely organized group of companions who called themselves the *Buveurs d'eau* ("the water drinkers," presumably because they could not afford wine, beer, or anything else alcoholic). They met in spaces found throughout the Nouvelle-Athènes neighborhood of the ninth arrondissement. A playwright named Théodore Barrière (1823–77) convinced Murger to help him adapt the stories for an 1849 theatrical production

titled *Bohemian Life* at the Théâtre des Variétés in Paris. The
production was an enormous success, which led Murger to
write additional "bohemian" stories and publish them in 1851.
In his preface to the volume, Murger described his subjects as

> a race of people who have existed in all climes and ages,
> and can claim an illustrious descent. They are the race of
> obstinate dreamers for whom art has remained a faith and
> not a profession .... The real Bohemians are really amongst
> those called by art, and have the chance of being also
> amongst its elect. [In] this Bohemia, two abysses flank it on
> either side—poverty and doubt.
>
> (Murger 1888: ii)

Murger had based the characters in his stories (and in the
play with Barrière) on his own experiences not only of poverty
and doubt, but also of deep friendships, young love, disease,
near-starvation, and death.

Bohemians thus became character types, not just characters
(most familiar later to audiences in two operas, one by Giacomo
Puccini in 1895 and another by Ruggero Leoncavallo in 1896,
but both titled *La Bohème*; the 1994 Broadway musical *Rent*
by Jonathan Larson also uses the Murger precedents for
the character types depicted). Such character types became
popular with their bourgeois opposites, who included lawyers,
physicians, real estate speculators, insurance brokers, bankers,
and even some clerks, tellers, cashiers, accountants, and
other "white collar" employees. The so-called "bohemians"
mocked the bourgeoisie, considering their values and habits
equally objectionable. Bohemians in the 1870s and 1880s
derided the bourgeois ideals of frugality, sobriety, celibacy,
and domesticity. Bourgeois Frenchmen, paradoxically, found
such accusations, along with the voluntary idiosyncrasies that
embraced destitution, insecurity poverty, and love affairs that
ended in death as objects of fascination. They avidly read
novels and stories like Murger's, and attended productions
like *Bohemian Life*. When certain bars, restaurants, and

similar venues became identified as bohemian gathering places, bourgeois curiosity prompted visits to such locales, where reputed bohemian exoticism, behaviors, affectations of dress, and peculiar manners of speech were on full display.

That bourgeois audiences flocked to bohemian displays has been a topic of fascination for decades, especially among students of both anthropology and the performing arts. For some observers, "bohemia" is a community within a community, a self-identifying aggregation of individuals who share sentiments of social marginality. They also share attitudes of metaphysical anxiety. The bourgeois, on the other hand, were mostly well-bred, well-fed, and well-bathed when they came to observe bohemians and to consume the entertainment packages they offered. Such consumers perhaps sought a release of feelings they most often sought to repress, or at least to experience something that was restricted in their everyday middle-class lives. But did the middle class really live in circumstances so restricted and confined that they needed some kind of eccentric behavior to reinvigorate themselves? Attempts to answer such questions can enkindle heated discussions in several directions, so for the purposes of these inquiries, the idea of a venue where "the increasingly organized and regulated life of the modern city could be left behind for an evening" must suffice. In such venues, non-Bohemians might seek release from ordinary social boundaries, experience the thrill of violating conventions, or acquaint themselves with assorted taboos (Seigel 1987: 240).

Among the first of such venues was the Café de la Rive Gauche in the "Latin Quarter" of the fifth and sixth arrondissements of Paris. This area got its name from the colleges located there, in which Latin remained the traditional language of instruction until the Revolution of 1789. There were numerous literary clubs that sprang up during the 1870s, but a group that called themselves *Les Hydropathes* ("the avoiders of water") became the precedent for subsequent cabaret efforts in Montmartre. Among the original members of the "Club des Hydropathes" were its President Èmile

Goudeau (1849–1906), along with Paul Arena (1843–96), Charles Cros (1824–88), Ernest Grenet-Dancourt (1854–1913), Jules Laforgue (1860–87), Maurice Mac-Nab (1856–89), Georges Rodenbach (1855–98), and Laurent Tailhade (1854–1919). This group was generally more prosperous than Mergur and his companions had been: not only did they drink wine, they had regular day jobs and lived in modest but comfortable dwellings. Not all of them were poets; some were musicians, performers, or artists. Their presentations became popular minor successes, with their work published in small-circulation journals and in Parisian newspapers.

The above-noted Goudeau (he was a clerk at the French Ministry of Finance) arranged for the lease of a large space in a nearby hotel in the Rue Cujas in the fifth arronidissement. His fellow Hydropathes possessed the resources to lease the space, which could accommodate about 300 people. At the Hydropathes Café, "cabaret" was on the menu. It was a round food platter encircled by wine bowls; it had been on the menus of taverns and *boîtes* for years in France. Food and bread were served on the round platter and wine drunk from bowls. The term came into more prominence as the group staged entertainments in the form of poetry or prose readings and songs. Their work became increasingly popular among audiences, and some of it was openly satirical, set to popular songs of the day. The increasing size of audiences at the biweekly gatherings indicated to Goudeau that some cultural changes were underway by the late 1870s.

The exercise became so popular that in January of 1879, Goudeau launched a bimonthly journal called *L'Hydropathe*, which published the work of several poets, essayists, and artists who had presented their work at the Hydropathes Café. By 1880, however, most of the adventurous energy that had animated both the club and the journal had dissipated. Groups within the original club formed breakaway organizations, calling themselves *Hirsutes* ("the hairy ones"), *Zutistes* ("the slackers"), and *Incohérents* ("the Incoherent Ones").

Rodolphe Salis

Louis Rodolphe Salis (1852–97) had been a frequent habitué of the Club Hydropathes, and his experiences there coincided with his desire to open a "cabaret artistique" in which poets presented their work for free to an audience willing to pay high prices for wine, cognac, and liqueur. To him, it seemed like a money-making proposition After a false start at a career as a painter, and with funds from his father and the dowry of his new (second) wife, Salis leased a small space in Montmartre that had been a post office. He thought it suitable for a *boîte* in the Boulevard Rochechouart. The place had only one advantage: it was near the Grande Pinte, one of the neighborhood's most popular taverns. Salis thought he might profit from any surplus in their customers. The neighborhood abounded in cats. After finding one that wanted to live in his home, Salis memorialized it in the name of his establishment, *Le Chat Noir.*

The interior of the place was eclectic in taste, to say the least. It looked like the kind of shop where pawnbrokers unloaded articles nobody would buy, and indeed some sources insist that Salis had filled the venue with cast-off tables and chairs he found discarded on the streets or in flea markets. Salis had little concern for the material milieu of his establishment, but rather for the literary and artistic atmosphere he hoped to create within it. Accounts vary about the first encounter between Salis and Goudeau, but the most credible include a chance meeting at the aforementioned Grande Pinte tavern in Montmartre. There a former member of the Hydropathes introduced Salis to Goudeau, and the former began to elaborate on his plans for a *cabaret artistique* in Montmartre. His most salient point was getting Goudeau to encourage former members of the Hydopathes to make the journey up to Montmartre and present their work to a live audience, just as they had done in the Latin Quarter. Goudeau immediately agreed, and in November 1881 Salis opened the Black Cat.

Directly in front of the establishment was a street light, and
Salis asked some former Hydropathes to stand under the light
for a while, giving the impression that the locale was popular.
A new bill-posting law permitted posters advertising the venue
to be pasted on vacant walls, tram waiting stations, and public
urinals. He also obtained permission from Parisian police to
have a piano on the premises. This, together with the printing
of a song book, encouraged customers to sing boisterously,
which created a need for much liquid refreshment. He then
began raising the prices of the beverages, which were mostly
spirits, aperitifs, and fortified wine. One of the *Chat Noir*'s first
musical performers was the former Hydropath member Jules
Jouy (1855–97), whose songs were often rousing critiques of
contemporary politicians or public figures.

Salis lit the interior of his venue with candles and oil lamps,
and their illumination provided ambience, enhancing the
special kind of atmosphere he wanted to create. There was also
a fairly large fireplace in one corner, supplementing warmth in
the cold winter months of 1882. As his income increased Salis
installed oak tables. Sketches of various Hydropaths hung on
the walls. Salis soon began publishing a small journal featuring
caricatures, sketches, song lyrics, poems, and essays by former
Hydropaths, along with others who were starting to appear
with greater frequency on the small platform stage Salis had
installed. The journal proved to be popular in Paris, further
stimulating attendance.

The establishment also benefited from a new trend that
found acceptance among certain numbers of the Parisian
bourgeoisie, who began to indulge themselves in an aperitif
before dinner even if one was not dining.[1] Crowds gathered at
the *Chat Noir*, which (as noted earlier) had ample supplies of
distillates and fortified wines. Salis dressed himself in a frock
coat, wearing a high stiff collar and spats on his shoes. He
furnished a small room at the back of the premises and set it
aside for his regular clientele and called it "the Institute." Salis
then developed another of his heretofore unknown talents, that
of a *conférencier*, or master of ceremonies. He interspersed

remarks and jokes of his own devising between the readings of poetry, the presentation of sketches, or musical offerings. He grandiloquently welcomed patrons as they came through the front door with mock salutations like "Ah! Your Honor—so glad to see you!" or "Somebody help His Excellency to his seat," or "Your Esteemed Electoral Highness, how nice of you to join us tonight!" Most of the performers at the *Chat Noir* resembled former Hydropaths or imitators of Hydropaths, telling stories about the poor and downtrodden in Paris, reciting verse in odd rhythmic structures, belting out songs called *chansons réalistes*, or sometimes staging dialogues in the nearly unintelligible gibberish of the street. Salis then launched a peculiarly eccentric political campaign to popularize visits to Montmartre and the *Chat Noir*. His electoral platform demanded the separation of Montmartre from France. "What is Montmartre?" he rhetorically asked. "Nothing. What should it be? Everything" (Appignanesi 2004: 15). Salis' campaign was nothing but a publicity stunt, but as such it attracted the attention of artists wanting to perform for free, while likewise enticing the paying public he sought as patrons.

One of the songs which premiered at the *Chat Noir* and later became popular was "An Old Workman," which celebrated the life of a broken-down vagrant with no place to spend the night. He notes that even dogs and pigs have places to sleep—but no matter. At least he doesn't have to pay rent. Songs with lyrics such as these became drawing cards to the *Chat Noir*, which in turn attracted talented songwriters like Jouy and Maurice Mac-Nab (1856–89) who had performed with the Hydropaths. Erik Satie (1866–1925) also worked for Salis when he took a forced leave of absence from the Paris Conservatory, the French national school of music. He ultimately led a small group of musicians for Salis, calling themselves the "Black Cat Orchestra." Salis and Satie, however, had several arguments over money and theirs was an unamicable parting.

Salis' most prolific songwriter was a lawyer named Leon Xanrof (Léon Alfred Fourneau, 1867–1953), who had no training in music but passed the French bar exam at age

twenty and was working for the Paris Court of Appeals
when he began to perform for Salis. Xanrof had grown up
in Montmartre, and his "songs without shame" (which he
called *Chansons sans gêne*) were often about the people of
the eighteenth arrondissement he had known since childhood.
His father had been a practicing physician whose clientele
included prostitutes, madams, pimps, and other disreputable
types. Xanrof became acquainted with several such individuals
when they visited his father's medical practice and he began
to chronicle the lives they led. During his long life (he died at
age eighty-six) he wrote over 3,000 chansons, such as "Les
Trottins" (Errand Girls), about poor working girls who dream
of love but who are most interested in money. It didn't matter
how or where they got it: a month in bed with a nice bachelor,
for example, was as good a route as any. In "Les Bohémes,"
Xanrof praised the disorderly dreamers of Montmartre, the
poets composing works while pondering the emptiness of their
wine glasses. Such, he sang, were "the favorites of the witless
bourgeoisie!" One day, the song explained, "the bohemians
will rise up. One day, I'll start working on my novel!" It was
a brilliant exercise in self-parody, though it also had a strong
dose of *épater la bourgeoisie*. It was a combination which
Xanrof often utilized, much to the enjoyment of his audiences,
who were growing steadily in number and in readiness to
spend disposable income on the drinks Salis offered.

As business continued to grow and prosper, Salis enriched
himself at the expense of performers and artists like Jouy and
Xanrof. His attitude toward them derived from Goudeau's
practice at the *Club Hydropathes*: performers and writers
obviously benefited from publicity the *Chat Noir* afforded
them, and he made no excuses for his policy of charging
performers for admission, just like ordinary customers. As
the crowds grew, Salis again raised the prices on his drinks
though he inaugurated a menu that offered small sandwiches and
cheeses. And in some ways, market forces were in his favor:
many of the songwriters enjoyed handsome profits from the
sale of sheet music to their songs. By some estimates, Parisians

bought sheet music for about 10,000 songs per year by the mid-1880s, and French copyright law provided royalty payments for every copy of any song published in France.[2]

As the lyrics of many Xanrof songs revealed, middle-class patrons enjoyed subject matter that treated the lives, experiences, and heartbreak of unglamorous, anonymous Parisians. Their experiences in seedy, crime-ridden neighborhoods, their modest ambitions, and the largely unremarkable events that happened to them every day somehow bore the stamp of non-threatening "authenticity" to bourgeois listeners. Perhaps they liked the songs because they could pretend to sympathize with the chanson's melodically manifested misery (Segal 1987: 42).

Aristide Bruant

Salis and the *Chat Noir* reached the apex of popularity with the debut of a singer/composer whom Jules Jouy brought to the venue in 1884 named Aristide Bruant (1851–1925). Jouy shared Bruant's enthusiasm for the rough nightlife in the seamy neighborhoods of Paris, and Bruant's first appearance on the small stage of the *Chat Noir*, depicting and glorifying "life in the gutter among the hookers and sluts," made a strong impression on his audiences (Kühn 1988: 81). He made the smug bourgeois his target, not only in his songs but in his patter between songs. It was as if he were putting them on trial, as if he were the legal advocate for the poor and the dispossessed. "So—you idiotic gluttons! What great piles of shit you are. Can't find a place to sit? Squeeze your fat cheeks in a little tighter on the bench, you self-satisfied dimwits!" (Kühn 1987: 15).

Bruant's mingling with and knowledge of Parisian outcasts was based on his own experience as a youth in the Paris slums near the Gare de Lyon railroad station and the nearby Mazas prison. He was fascinated with Parisian street life, its neighborhoods, many of its most unfortunate denizens, and particularly with the way they talked. Their argot was "colorful, animated, brutal, cynical, but rich in picturesque metaphors, bold in neologisms, and imitative in harmonies" (Bruant 1972: 45). Born in the tiny town of Courteney, Bruant left for Paris at age fifteen, eventually getting a well-paid job as a clerk with the French Northern Railroad. He then began augmenting his clerk's income by singing songs of his own composition (both lyrics and music) in café-concerts. Among his first engagements was at the Concert des Amandandiers in the Parisian district of Belleville.[3]

In his songs at café-concerts he developed the persona of a jobless former soldier working as a day laborer in the hope of finding a steady job. It was a familiar type among some café-concert performers, but what made Bruant (see Figure 1) distinctive was his manner of dress, which soon became his trademark costume: black corduroy suit, trousers tucked into heavy black boots, a red flannel shirt, a large black hat, a long red scarf, a walking stick, and at times a black cape. Bruant's sartorial self-fashioning was the first evidence of distinguishing himself from both his audience and his fellow performers. Comparing his outfit to those of other café-concert performers, one can detect how eccentricity worked in his favor. His wardrobe did not conform with contemporary ideas of what a young working-class man should look like. It was in fact somewhat extravagant: the tucked-in boots made him look like he had arrived on a horse; the long red scarf looked far more expensive than the kind of neckwear a common worker could afford. There was solidity in the black suit with the black cape, topped with a wide-brimmed black hat. And then there was that preposterous, pseudo-sophisticated walking stick, but all were vital to Bruant's self-presentation. It placed him outside the bounds of most public entertainers at the time. It was part of Bruant's intention: he was not interested in becoming a public entertainer anyway. He wanted to become a public personality.

His desire for renown led to a split with Salis, whose success with the *Chat Noir* prompted him to look for another building which might accommodate his expanding audience.

Figure 1 *Aristide Bruant, ca. 1886, anonymous. Courtesy of Alamy Stock Photo.*

He found the property he wanted in the Rue Laval, what is today the Rue Victor-Massé, only about four blocks south of the original *Chat Noir*. It was a sumptuous old private mansion belonging to the Belgian painter Alfred Stevens (1823–1906).

Bruant then rented the former *Chat Noir* for himself and renamed it *Le Mirliton*. His approach to operating a cabaret differed substantially from the method Salis employed. The name *Le Mirliton*, for example, was intentional because its literal meaning was "reed pipe" but it also connoted "doggerel"—a form of cheap verse with trivial meaning—which could describe most of what Bruant wrote. The new management wanted to emphasize his connection to and sympathy with the Parisian down-and-out. Few other venues in Paris made that attempt, but *Le Mirliton* also focused on aspects of Bruant's persona. *Le Mirliton* was furthermore open only for very limited amounts of time: usually from 10:00 p.m. to midnight. Such limitations, Bruant correctly surmised, conveyed the idea of his presence as a limited commodity, thereby attracting bigger crowds. He periodically stayed open till 2:00 a.m. because it made him more money. And entry was selective. Customers had to knock at the venue's front door and supply reasons for their desire for admission. Once inside, Bruant pursued the aggressive style of greeting he had initiated when he worked for Salis, only now he had become offensive, as he subjected his customers to a fusillade of insults:

Look what we have here, gentlemen—look at these girls tonight! Whores to be sure, but some real beauties among them! For the love of God, look at them. No bidet slops, no sir. We have real trollops of choice tonight, deluxe courtesans in the flesh! And take a look at the monsieur following behind that one. He must be a pimp. Or maybe an ambassador ....

The crowd loved it, and it may somehow have set in motion the tendency of future cabaret performers to deprecate members of their audience.

Bruant, however, had more than just his persona for sale. He had ample supplies of sheet music, along with broadsides that printed his lyrics, his observations, his "philosophy," and his ideas. The only drink available at *Le Mirliton* was beer, though Bruant engaged in the curious practice of individual pricing. Customers paid different prices for the same beverage. Prices varied from customer to customer, and Bruant condemned customers who allowed their glasses to run empty. Like Salis, Bruant engaged in banter with customers, and he often interspersed his musical numbers with demands that customers buy copies of his sheet music and his pamphlets. Those who chose to leave, at whatever point in the evening, were his targets of special invective, sung out of the establishment with a chorus of "All customers are pigs, especially those who leave early."

Such epithets convinced his hearers that Bruant was indeed a genius and a true evocation of Parisian street life. "You're on the street?" he rhetorically asked. "You're already at home." The implication was that life on the street and the poverty, disease, and violence that came with it were somehow acts of defiance against bourgeois norms. Life on the street, as the title (*Dans le rue*) of his 1889 collection of chansons and monologues indicated, had provided him with authority to become the creator *sans pareil* of the *chanson réaliste*.

As Jerrold Seigel has noted, Bruant may have harbored personal contempt for the well-dressed, well-fed, and well-bathed customers who entered his establishment. But the insults he heaped upon them were actually forms of complimentary greeting. He realized that coming to *Le Mirliton* in Montmartre was a form of what today is called "slumming," a term already in use among New Yorkers in 1884 (Lee 2009; also Heap 2009: 2). It was a "voyeuristic pastime" in New York and London for the well-heeled to visit crime-ridden, somewhat notorious and decrepit neighborhoods. Some believe that Bruant's appeal lay in his ability to become the substitute voice of the downtrodden and oppressed. When his songs and routines explicitly treated politics, he switched

over to mockery. For example, one of his lyrics spoke of a
street cleaner who self-identified as a socialist, but he conceded
that he knew nothing about politics and in any case he could
understand nothing of what the socialist speakers had to say at
factory gates or at rallies he attended (Seigel 1986: 237). Most
of Bruant's subjects did not have jobs at all: they were what
Marx and Engels had called the *Lumpenproletariat*, illiterate
members "of the lowest social strata in society, insensible to
calls for revolution and who usually were nothing more than
the bribed tools of reactionary intrigue" (Marx and Engels
1848: 49). They were the tattered and tired, the homeless, the
diseased and degenerate, the huddled masses who exploited
each other and who got in trouble with the police. A common
theme among Bruant's subjects was figuring out where to sleep
at night. In the lives of these individuals, Bruant discovered
sudden outbreaks of fear, love, jealousy, violence, and revenge.
He advocated no political action on their behalf, and his
stance toward them was almost romantic. His attraction for
"the brutish and animalistic underside of modern life" was
borne of his conviction that he had risen above it.

Two good examples of Bruant's subjects and his approach
to them are the ballad lyrics for "A Batignolles" and "A St.
Lazare." The former presents the voice of a girl named Flora,
who fell into prostitution at an early age. She grew up in
Batignolles, a Paris neighborhood located in the seventeenth
arrondissement, just west of Montmartre. Like Montmartre,
Batignolles was an independent village until 1860 when, like
Montmartre, the national government annexed it and made it
part of Paris. It was a tough place in which to grow up, and it
had no fashionable bohemian literary profile. Flora was native
to Batignolles, and Bruant infers that her fate was almost
inevitable: "Her mama called her Flora, she never knew her
papa. So young when she attended school at Batignolles. She
sprouted up like a mushroom, despite getting slapped around
at night at Batignolles. I loved her as much as I could, but then
she deceived me with Anatole at Batignolles." That is the song's
hook: the song is not really about Flora but about the speaker,

who is her pimp. Inevitably, he says, "It had to happen, sooner or later, 'cuz Anatole is such a sneak … And now she's left me, but God gave me my revenge: she's going to die of the pox at Batignolles." Bruant holds the neighborhood responsible for her fate, not the pimp. But what is a girl to do?

In "À Saint-Lazare" (In the St. Lazare Prison) Bruant assumes the persona of a prostitute whom the Parisian health authorities accuse of contracting and spreading syphilis. They have confined her to the infirmary of the St. Lazare Prison, and the song is a letter to her pimp.

> In Ste. Lazare I'm writing you, my poor Polyte. Little did I suspect that my visit to the doctor yesterday would land me in prison. I had no idea that I had the disease, which means I can no longer work the streets, now that I'm at Saint-Lazare! But during this time, my dear, what will you do? I can't send you anything, 'cuz here, everyone is broke. It takes three months to make just twenty sous at Saint-Lazare!

She offers her goodbyes to Polyte and wishes him well. Find another girl who will care for you, she says, and tell her I am grateful. "I embrace you, my love, even though I know you're not the caressing type. But now I must go to communion at Sainte-Marguerite."

Such songs gave audiences a good feeling about themselves, because unlike her Polyte, they had sympathy for her. Bruant's strategy was to expose the lot of prostitutes and accuse the good gentlemen in the audience, God-fearing and respectable, of perpetuating such suffering by paying for her services. These lovely gentlemen, Bruant infers, are no different from pimps like Polyte. And the good gentlemen applauded the accusation, because in their heart of hearts they knew they were not like Polyte. True, the girl's plight is regrettable. But they bore no responsibility for it. They were saddened by it, and that was enough. After all, the girl says she must now go to Sainte-Marguerite, which is both a church and a cemetery.

Bruant also wrote numerous execution songs, which had a lengthy history, dating as far back as the seventeenth century. They were usually grisly chronicles of the condemned's deeds. Most such songs were the products of town criers, who sang of crimes, hangings, and other incidents in the town's life, perhaps best understood as precursors of today's news media (Fritzsche 1996: 16). They usually included the criminal's admission of regret, which carried implicit moralizing. Into this kind of tradition Aristide Bruant insinuated himself. In his "Á la Roquette" (At Roquette Prison), he composed a description of the convict's inner struggles and his fears about the coming morning when he will lose his head.

> As I shout out these words, my guts cannot be controlled. My head juts through a round opening. Since midnight I've been wide-awake … I hear the kind of noise they make when guillotining. Before they cut my neck they slice my collar here. And then I see the shear's cold blade, through my shirt careening. I feel so chilly and afraid at guillotining.

Bruant's critics claimed such graphic portrayals were patronizing, because it clearly assigned blame and responsibility to the condemned. Attitudes in response to such accusations had a mixed effect on his large audience, who flocked to Montmartre for an evening of "slumming" and a side dish of self-congratulation. Some praised Bruant as a genuine critic of the status quo, one who genuinely opposed the exploitation of the *miséreux*. Others pilloried him as an opportunist who knew that songs of crime and lowlifes sold well. His strategy at *Le Mirliton*, his accusers claimed, was nothing more than "bourgeois-bohemianism" (Sonn 1989: 133). Bruant himself was somewhat equivocal, voicing contempt for both sides:

> [Those] idiots do not understand what I sing to them, [they] cannot understand, not knowing what it is to die from hunger, those who have come to the world with a silver spoon in their mouths. I avenge myself in insulting,

in treating them worse than dogs. That makes them laugh to the point of tears. They believe that I joke when, often enough, it is a breeze from the past, misery submitted to, dirtiness seen, which re-mounts on my lips and makes me speak as I do.

(in Sonn 1989: 131)

But Bruant used scathing terms for pimps, those "sodomites" who give (or take) it "up the ass" (Hérail and Lovatt 1984: 187). In his *L'argot au XXc siècle* (French Argot of the Twentieth Century) he cited dozens of slang terms for prostitutes and pimps; his ballad "Marche de dos" depicts pimps who celebrate the good fortune of having a "good woman earner," though he uses the term *marmite*, which is a kind of cooking pan (Bruant and Bercy 1905: 310). Bruant sometimes depicted pimps as sponges or parasites who viewed johns as dupes ripe for the picking, easy marks for robbery or other forms of criminal abuse. And the police (like most forms of government) were always intruding into their world. In Bruant's world, sex was for sale or purchase on the street market, like any other commodity. Most sexual encounters took place on back streets, alleys, or even doorways. Very few occurred in brothels, and in most cases the woman's job was to accommodate, not respond. There is as a result a bitter irony in many Bruant songs, since the conflict is often between the prostitute and her pimp. No pimp is interested in social mobility, and no streetwalker aspires to the level of courtesan or call girl. No pimp is ever held accountable for a prostitute's situation. In fact, the pimp often encourages the hooker to bring in more business. The reason? The pimp aspires to the status of rent-seeker: he abhors the idea of a regular job or even worse, a respectable occupation. His goal is to keep his woman on the street, working for him. His badges of honor are laziness, asocial violence, exploitation, male virility, and a cynical knowledge of life in the streets. Such a figure was a hero among the down-and-outs, the *miséreux*.

Yvette Guilbert

Emma Laure Esther Guilbert (1865–1944) was the second (behind Bruant) great "discovery" which Leon Xanrof brought to the cabaret public. She began singing as a child in the streets of her native Paris, and by age sixteen she was working as a model of women's apparel in one of the larger Parisian department stores, Printemps. Like Bruant, she began her singing career in café-concerts. By the time she was nineteen, Xanrof brought her to Bruant, who found her "worthy" of singing songs he wrote for her (the best example of which is "A Saint-Ouèn"). She began to earn substantial sums as a singer in large venues not only in Montmartre but also throughout Paris and on tour. Also like Bruant, she became immortalized in posters by Henri Toulouse-Lautrec.

The posters preceded her on an 1896 tour of the United States, as did her reputation for singing "naughty" songs very few Americans could understand. Fascinating to French audiences, she scandalized others with her persona of the gaunt, working-class girl who was a slut but didn't mind reciting the story of how she became one. In fact, she reveled in the telling. The *Los Angeles Herald* headlined the newspaper's review of her 1896 concert in Chicago with "Naughty Yvette Guilbert," but then proceeded to echo many French critics who praised her ability "to make obscenities palatable by uttering them with a nonchalant air." Her novelty was to create the illusion of innocence while delivering the most risqué verses imaginable. Her voice had a "hard, tin-pan quality," a result, said the reviewer of "the effort to make herself heard above the chatter of the drinking throng, the clink of glasses and the cries of waiters" in venues like cabarets. The Los Angeles critic praised Guilbert (see Figure 2) as "the new thing–the real and true artist in a great many ways." Her magnetism was undeniable, he said. You can't look at anything or anyone else when she sings about wretched drunkards in the Parisian streets, or the so-called virgins who come to Paris fresh from the convent with

Figure 2 *Yvette Guilbert, ca. 1900, anonymous. Courtesy of Alamy Stock Photo.*

intimate knowledge of sin under a pious exterior. By American
standards, nearly every one of Guilbert's songs was grossly
improper. But since nobody in the Chicago crowd could
understand French, "not much injury will be done to your
modesty by anything you will hear from this singer, be it never
so fragile a Cook County flower" (*Los Angeles Herald* 1896).

Guilbert's vocal work, like Bruant's, had a substantial
impact on the subsequent practice of song delivery in most
cabaret venues. According to Hans-Peter Bayerdörfer, Yvette
Guilbert created the image of the cabaret *diseuse* and raised
the aesthetic expectations for both French and German female
singers. After Guilbert, no cabaret *diseuse* fit into traditional
vocal categories. There were no lyric sopranos, no spintos,
no contraltos, no soubrettes in cabaret. The use of extreme
pitches, from low to high and back again in the same song,
was customary. So was the technique of alternating talk with
singing. So was the abrupt switching from one rhythmic
sequence, or time signature, to another within the same song.
And there were divisions within spoken parts of the song:
some portions lachrymose, some portions descriptive, others
declaimed, others prosaic in the extreme.

It was also important for the *diseuse* in cabaret to maintain
body posture, to forge a kind of silhouette in the audience's
mind. That meant starting a song off-key with very little
movement and almost with an inaudible whisper. As the song
progressed, Guilbert said, the use of the arms was important,
from stretching upwards to the ceiling to outwards, as if to
embrace someone. The most effective stance, according to one
eye-witness who saw Guilbert's work in Paris, was one that
somehow combined "the half-wilted, pathetic coquette with
the other half, a stern English governess" (Klossowski 1903:
51). With the celebrity status accorded to Bruant and Guilbert,
modern cabaret had arrived definitively as a form, with its
characteristic spaces, treatment of the audience, performed
materials, and constructed personae. From here it was to
develop the model in a different context.

2

The Craze Spreads to Germany

Kabarett

Establishing cabaret in German-speaking Europe was a conscious, deliberate undertaking. Unlike the *Chat Noir* in Montmartre, German cabaret was the product of intentional duplication, coupled with a longing for some kind of reduction in scale. "Small is beautiful" was embedded in the term *Brettl* ("little boards)" used within a cabaret context, intentionally contrasting it with *Bretter* ("boards"), the metaphorical term Friedrich Schiller (1759–1805) deployed in an 1803 poem to describe a theater stage. It also represented a longing among many German intellectuals for a release from entrenched traditions of prudery and censorship. Finally, it was an elitist undertaking, but at the same time it manifested a vulgar appeal. A prolific writer named Otto Julius Bierbaum (1865–1910) had outlined what a German-language cabaret should look like in his 1897 novel *Stilpe*: "a kind of rude music hall that satisfied a naked lust for beauty and a sense of humor that takes the world by the scruff of the neck" (Bierbaum 1901: 15). In Bierbaum's view, cabaret was to capture the ideal of a "chamber theatre" in which audience and performer shared a fairly small space, allowing a relatively small group of people sharing a small space to escape the constraints of Victorian/Wilhelmine philistinism.

The German tours of Yvette Guilbert in the 1890s, along with the Paris World's Fair in 1899, had awakened German interest in cabaret. But Bierbaum realized that the provocative style present in French cabaret would not easily transfer to Germany—particularly not in Prussia and its capital Berlin, where a stringent censorship was in force. A good solution, he thought, might be an artistic upgrade of the German *Variété* entertainment. German *Variété* was popular among audiences and police censors generally regarded it as harmless. Bierbaum imagined something a bit naughtier, perhaps along the lines of Guilbert's performances. He was a good friend of the controversial pundit Oskar Panizza,[1] who had long advocated women in short skirts and their use of face powder, lipstick, rouge, and mascara in public as cultural weapons against prevailing philistine tastes in Berlin (Panizza 1898). Bierbaum had already made that argument in his novel *Stilpe*, claiming that "in the lacy panties of my sweet little girl is hidden more lyricism than in your entire *Collected Works*. And when the time is right, she won't have to wear anything at all. When she dances I am inspired to write poetry! My [ideal] cabaret is named for Momus, after all, the personification of satire and mockery" (1901: 377). Bierbaum in 1900 published a collection titled *German Chansons,* whose initial printing sold out quickly. The chansons spoke of a hypothetical "Variété of the Future," which was to be an "aesthetic institution" to re-invigorate the German mind in the spirit of Friedrich Nietzsche. In his interpretation of Nietzsche, the editor and pundit Herwarth Walden (1879–1941) described the ideal cabaret as one "with a cultural task before it—and it must not shirk its duty: it must always look for stylistic unity within a small setting, while at the same time offer full and complete shapes and figures" (in Sprengel 1998: 155). "We want to raise the standards of taste," Bierbaum agreed. "We want to write poetry that is not read in quiet chambers .... Our motto is 'applied lyrics,' and in our opinion only when applied is art any good" (Bierbaum 1900: x).

A minor aristocrat named Baron Ernst von Wolzogen (1855–1934) took as his mission the establishment of a cabaret that combined the "applied" poetics of Bierbaum and the "mission" Nietzsche might have imagined. Wolzogen also wanted to borrow features of the *Chat Noir* and *Le Mirliton* in Montmartre; he had visited both during a visit to the 1899 Paris World's Fair. To him, the "ideal" cabaret was a venue where bohemians gathered to hear songs of praise about women whose power transcended the perimeters of bourgeois limitations. Wolzogen saw himself as a combination of Rudolphe Salis and Aristide Bruant, serving as an interlocutor between songs and the presentation of poetry. It was an *Überbrettl*, borrowing the Nietzschen prefix *über* to convey the ideal of rising above the confines of traditional bourgeois narrow-mindedness. The aforementioned *Brettl* signified a "higher calling" of legitimacy to variety shows (such as those at the aforementioned Varieté). *Überbrettl* was thus a neologism with a complicated provenance, but Wolzogen was himself a man with complicated aesthetic perceptions. His goal was to embellish *Varieté* and its bastard cousin *Tingel-Tangel*[2] with a patina of artistic tenability in a venue where "the entertainment needs of our fellow human beings are actually being justified, whereas previously they have uniformly been denounced as non-art" (Bierbaum 1900: ix).

By the time he founded his *Überbrettl*, Ernst von Wolzogen was already a published author of several erotic novels including *Stories of Sweet Young Girls* (1898), *The Third Sex* (1899), and *A Royal Wench* (1900). He was the grandson of a Prussian general, the son of a theater's managing director, and the putative great-grandnephew of playwright and poet Friedrich Schiller (1759–1805). In 1892 Wolzogen had founded the Independent Literary Society in Munich and later became the director of the "Academic-Dramatic Society" in Berlin. A Prussian patriot, he opened the *Überbrettl* on January 18, 1901, the 200th anniversary of the Prussian

Kingdom's founding. He arrayed himself as a preposterous dandy, looking like a middle-aged playboy, introducing several ladies as his companions, whom he had conveniently hired for the occasion (Wolzogen 1908: 238). He mounted the stage and played the German version of Rodolphe Salis and a little bit of Bruant (whose singing style he unsuccessfully tried to imitate). Between musical numbers of actors he had hired to sing, do poetry readings, and create dialogue sketches, Wolzogen offered observations and introduced performers.

His novels had revealed Wolzogen as a man with preoccupations concerning certain kinds of women. Fascinated by both feminists and lesbians, he was also a firm supporter of the Kaiser and Prussia; in 1914 he was a vocal advocate of the German duty to wage war against both Russia and France and in 1920 joined the new Nazi Party. In 1900 Wolzogen persuaded various people to loan him sums of 500–1,000 Reichsmarks (RM), and by January 1901 had collected RM 10,000 (mostly from Jewish investors, he later claimed), but this sum did not permit him to realize his goal of renting a theater in a fashionable quarter of Berlin. He had to settle instead for a lease on the somewhat seedy premises of a bankrupt venue in a working-class district near Alexander Platz, some distance from the entertainment center of Berlin. The opening night of Wolzogen's theater (which according to official documents he titled the *Buntes*, or "Colorful" Theater) was a smashing success. The entire evening went on for over three hours, which provided a "colorful" mixture of moods and genres.

Wolzogen's premiere was so successful that it started an avalanche of cabarets in Berlin; it later became known as the "cabaret epidemic" among critics and audiences, because so many bars, taverns, and beer gardens began to feature "cabaret-style" entertainment. The Colorful Theater was sold out for several weeks, allowing Wolzogen to pay off his investors only ten days after the premiere. Critical response in most of Berlin's ninety-three newspapers was positive, and many critics praised Wolzogen for his versatility as a master of ceremonies. The undertaking made such a stir in

Berlin that tickets for the first twenty performances became a positive investment. At one time they actually went up to RM 200 each. By the summer of 1901, Berlin police reported that they had received an additional forty-two petitions to open cabarets, a sign that some kind of craze had developed.[3] Department stores introduced the "cabaret look" for men's and women's fashions in their display windows. Wolzogen organized tours of his shows to cover most of the German Reich by train, and some tours even reached faraway outposts in the east like Romania and Bulgaria. Wolzogen had thus unintentionally inaugurated two new German professions: the performing master of ceremonies and the enterprising cabaret entrepreneur. By the end of 1901, forty new Berlin cabaret venues had sprouted. In October of 1901 the painter and costume designer Max Tilkes (1869–1942) opened his *Kabarett zum hungrigen Pegasus* (The Hungry Pegasus), featuring himself on guitar. On that occasion Tilke's friend Ernst Griebel joined him on the banjo and they sang duets of what they innocently termed "niggersongs." In early 1902 the painter Georg David Schulz (1865–1910) opened his *Im siebenten Himmel* (Seventh Heaven). Soon *Trianon*, *Die grüne Minna* (the Paddy Wagon), *Schminkschatulle* (the Powder Puff), *Die silberne Punschterine* (the Silver Punch Bowl), and many others opened for business.

The atmosphere, architecture, and general layout of most Berlin cabarets differed substantially from their Parisian precedents. In Paris, audience members were encouraged to drink and smoke during performances. They conversed with each other and observed very few formalities normally expected among audiences. There was a directness and an intimacy between performer and public. In contrast, many of the early cabaret venues in Berlin retained the traditional arrangement of audience members sitting in rows facing the stage, watching hired actors perform the material. German patrons certainly smoked and drank, but only in the theater lobby. Moreover, patrons had to buy tickets in advance and arrive punctually. They then were expected to view and listen attentively, which in subsequent retrospective seems "anti-cabaret." But it accomplished what Wolzogen, Bierbaum, and others had demanded: a *Varieté* with artistic and cultural embellishments, a *Tingel-Tangel* with class.

Of the many imitators Wolzogen spawned, one of the more significant was the *Schall und Rauch* (Noise and Smoke) of Max Reinhardt. Schall und Rauch took its name from the garden scene in Goethe's *Faust* I, in which Faust tells Gretchen, *Gefühl ist alles; der Name ist Schall und Rauch, umnebelnd Himmelsglut* ("Feeling is everything. The name is noise and smoke, befogging the glowing heavens"). Reinhardt was at the time a young character actor at Otto Brahm's Deutsches Theater, who with other actors had formed a kind of club called *Die Brille* (The Spectacles). Reinhardt and his colleagues, like Bierbaum and Wolzogen, shared a distaste for Wilhelmine philistinism. But Reinhardt decided that a "parody theatre" was the best path toward a small stage style that broke with the restrictions and hindrances which the Berlin police department seemed so eager to enforce. Reinhardt and his pals rented the Künstlerhaus in Bellevue Strasse and did parodies of Schiller's *Don Carlos* (titled "Charlie, a Thieves' Carnival"), Maeterlinck's *Pelleas and Melisande* (titled "Carleas and Elisande"), *The Oresteia* of Aeschylus (as "The Diarrhesiae of Persiflegels"), and other spoofs which appealed to an admittedly elite audience. Noise and Smoke also featured original sketches, like the double act called "Serenissimus und Kindermann," which featured caricatures of two distinctly minor officials from the Kaiser's court. Neither Serenissimus nor Kindermann knew anything about the performing arts, and they knew even less about cabaret. Yet they occupied what appeared to be the Kaiser's exclusive box seats in a theater somewhere. They personified the well-known dimwittedness of the German ruling elites, but in the process the performers who played them ran the risk of arrest for *lèse majesté* at nearly every performance.

One of the actors in the group, Rudolf Bernauer, soon dropped out and founded a program of his own with Carl

Meinhard; they called themselves *Die bösen Buben* (The Bad Boys). They also did parodies of current shows in Berlin. But Bernauer wanted to do more than just parody. In one sketch he and Meinhard posed as juvenile escapees from Berlin's Moabit jail. Meinhard did most of the sketch writing, while Bernauer did most of the comic setups. Their act evolved into a routine in which both boys regaled the audience with tales of their encounters with police, school officials, and other figures of authority. Their biggest hit was "Song of the Bad Boys," which not only sold sheet music by the thousands but became their theme song, sung at the close of their shows. "We just knocked over the cashier's desk, cleaned him out completely. They let us go because we're still in school / And because we dress so neatly. If some wise guy comes along, we knock him 'til he's senseless. And all the time we're feeling fine: we're psychologically defenseless!"

Like Reinhardt, Bernauer (1880–1953) was an Austrian who brought with him a distinct Viennese and somewhat warped feel for comedy, but he hoped to establish himself in the north German metropolis "among the blue eyes," as he called Berliners. Bernauer became a genuine Berliner in a very short period of time—a phenomenon that was the subject of his hit comedy of 1909 called *Einer von unser Leut* (One of Our Kind). Also like Reinhardt, Bernauer had no "respectable" education. He came from a lower-middle-class background, and his parents were immigrants from Hungary. As a teenager, Bernauer discovered that show business could be not only a means to gain respectability, but also a way to make good money in the process. His first jobs in Berlin included working for Wolzogen at the Colorful Theater, where he met both Meinhard and Reinhardt. Many of the great Berlin actors, Bernauer claimed, got their start in Berlin as comedians in such cabarets (Bernauer 1955: 110). With their non-blue eyes always on the "main chance," Bernauer and Meinhard tried repeatedly to get their own venue started, even as they worked for Reinhardt. They played balls and other such large soirées in order to get their act more well known.

Several theaters regularly went dark in the summer, so
Bernauer concentrated on working out a sub-lease. He
found several, but none were successful enough for him to
locate a permanent venue until 1911, when they took over
the Hebbel Theater in what is today the Stresemann Strasse.
There, Bernauer claims to have given Marlene Dietrich her
stage debut in 1917 (when she was sixteen) in a play called
When the New Wine Ripens by Björnsterne Björnson. It was
a comedy about a domineering mother who locates husbands
for her three daughters when they reach marriageable age. By
then, Bernauer had left the cabaret business and was working
full time as a comic director and playwright.[4]

Munich

Three months after Wolzogen opened his Colorful Theater,
a company of actors, writers, and performers in Munich
calling themselves the *Elf Scharfrichter* (Eleven Executioners)
began operations in a small space behind the Gasthaus zum
goldenen Hirsch (Golden Stag Hotel) and Restaurant in the
Schwabing district of Munich. Unlike Wolzogen's Colorful
Theater, theirs was a group-directed effort. The founders
(among whom was the Frenchman Marc Henry, who had
worked in Montmartre before arriving in Munich with his
Franco-German girlfriend, Marya Delvard) included actor
Otto Falckenberg (1873–1947) and sketch writer Leo Greiner
(1876–1928). Falckenberg and Greiner raised RM 200 to rent
the Hirsch Hotel space. Other members of the group had little
trouble raising the RM 1,000 for the initial lease, because some
of them came from affluent families. Others were established
writers or painters, working full-time and earning salaries.
Robert Kothe was a practicing attorney; fellow Executioner
Max Langheinrich was a working architect with a firm in
Munich. He agreed to transform the space into a working
theater, and renovations began in late 1900.

The Executioners based their name on their opposition to a bill in the German national parliament (Reichstag) called the Lex Heinze or "Heinze Law." The proposed law was intended to criminalize pimping but contained riders which banned frank depiction of sexual subject matter in print, severely penalized publishing and selling prurient literature, forbade the public display of immoral art works, and disallowed any public performance of lewd behavior. The Lex Heinze bill was defeated, but it aroused the ire of speech and press freedom advocates, such as the founders and supporters of Eleven Executioners.

In 1900, when the Executioners began to rehearse in their new space, Munich was the largest city in Bavaria. It was largely Catholic, and parts of it (such as the aforementioned Schwabing district) had a reputation for relative tolerance. Other parts were crime-ridden, beset with public drunkenness, prostitution, idleness, disease, vagrancy, and pimping. Official responses to criminality were usually harsh, especially after the national penal code took effect in 1871. A "national contagious diseases statute" allowed police to quarantine buildings or even whole districts in neighborhoods that seemed to breed tuberculosis, typhoid, and cholera. Few such undesirable neighborhoods had electric lighting or indoor plumbing, and crime rates in such areas were high when Bavaria became a constituent part of the new empire (Abrams 1988).

Munich also had a tradition of Shrovetide merriment, called *Fasching*. It was a medieval tradition that featured revelry leading up to Ash Wednesday. During Shrovetide, although such things were in reality rare, the character of the public executioner and his assistants, all bearing instruments of torture and death, showed up with regularity. Some Munich revelers in the late 1890s proclaimed themselves "The Criminals," impersonating murderers and thieves. "They brought a carnival atmosphere to their own Lex Heinze Parade through the Munich streets," Jennifer Ham has noted. But "not for the purpose of advocating [criminality], but to spoof government attempts [such as the Lex Heinze legislation] to suppress artistic freedom" (Ham 2000: 41). The rise of cabaret in Munich is thus tied closely to social uses and customs, but also to the dual appreciation of crime and punishment. Cabaret in Munich is also connected to the work and person of playwright Frank Wedekind, one of the most well-known members of the Eleven Executioners, whose songs about crime and punishment became more popular and lucrative for him than did his plays.

The Executioners' cabaret was located at Türken Strasse 28, between a saddler's shop and the workshop of a casket maker. Architect Langheinrich began his work by creating a raised stage at one end of the hall and installing a house curtain. He also constructed a small but usable backstage space, which served as a workshop in which members constructed wings, properties, and repaired lighting instruments. Perhaps most important to the group's subsequent success was Langheinrich's design and installation of new electrical circuits to facilitate lighting effects. The Eleven Executioners became one of the first cabarets in Germany to deploy lighting effects to enhance their performances. There was also an upstairs space which served as an office and dressing room.

In the midst of the audience Langheinrich installed a "pillory of shame," to which the Executioners had nailed legislative proposals, court orders, and police regulations from the Munich censorship office. Over the pillory hung an apparently decapitated head, which wore a judge's horsehair wig. The Türken Strasse venue accommodated 100 patrons at most, seated at tables and chairs. On the walls hung caricatures of each Executioner's head, along with lithographs, sketches, and drawings. The group called their performances "executions," which they scheduled three times weekly. Tickets for the shows cost RM 3, and patrons could reserve tickets in advance. The Executioners made a grand opening dressed in red cassocks and hoods, wearing black masks, and each carrying an executioner's axe (though some photographs depict them carrying swords). They immediately broke into songs taken from Bierbaum's *German Chansons*, which

Henry introduced and to which he added commentary. One eye-witness described Henry as extraordinarily bright, witty, and amusing. His French-accented German was hilarious, and he made the most of it as the group's master of ceremonies. Munich audiences "took him to their hearts rapturously," even as he attacked Bavarian philistinism and the Munich police in his routines (Stern 1951: 28).

The debut of Marya Delvard, the group's only female member, was literally electric. The costume dress she planned to wear ripped in half shortly before she was to go on, so she changed into her street clothes, which fit her snugly. Backstage, Marc Henry pinned it even more snugly around her body, which was already fairly svelte. The lights went down and then came up on her in a purple glow, which emphasized the bleached look of her face and the sheen of her red hair as she looked up into the light. "The whole place dissolved into a quiet gasp, as she seemed to have risen from a burial plot. There was not a sound in the place, not a sound from glass or dish. The only thing that came to mind was the vision of a vampire wasting away from all her sins, grappling with the cruelty of death" (Carossa 1928: 88).

She sang Wedekind's "Ilse," about a fifteen-year-old girl who fell into the joys of forbidden love and didn't want to quit. "And when my days of love are over, I'll go gladly to my grave," she sang. Delvard had a vampirish, demonic effect, and at the same time she appeared delicate and easily broken. That was her special charm, according to Hanns Gumppenberg, namely "the contradiction between *femme fatale* and *femme fragile*. She was not the perpetrator but the victim. She came across as sickly, weak, childlike, tender, yet with aristocratic tendencies." Gumppenberg was himself a decayed aristocrat, so perhaps he recognized in her performance something uncomfortably familiar: "A corrupt world has broken her, and she goes down with it. Thus a light vapor of death surrounds her" (Gumppenberg 1929: 282). The fact that Delvard hid her legal marriage to Marc Henry helped them both to maintain her public image as a bohemian woman, disregarding the strictures of Wilhelminian society by living apparently in sin with her equally sinful partner. The revelation that she was a respectable lady would clearly have damaged her.

Six weeks later, Wedekind joined the group at their invitation. Since Delvard and others were singing his songs to great effect, he wanted to sing them himself. By way of introducing himself, Wedekind announced to the audience, "Let me say first of all that I'm singing songs allowed by the police. Later I'll sing the ones they prohibited" (Forcht 2009: 63). Soon thereafter the Executioners raised the price of admission when he performed to RM 10, and later they charged RM 30, so great was his notoriety. By January 1902 he claimed that he was making more money from his cabaret performances than he ever made as a playwright. But then, he was earning very little as a playwright, though he did receive royalties from published versions of his plays. He received nothing from cabaret performances by others of his songs, which is ironic in view of the use Marya Delvard made of them. Despite critical acclaim and selling out most nights for three years, the group went bankrupt (and disbanded in the fall of 1904). Yet they had established several precedents for German cabaret, perhaps most notable among them the personality of Delvard as a *diseuse*. She sang not only Wedekind songs: she proved to be a superb interpreter of Weinhöppel's "bandit ballads" as well as an expert expositor of linguistically exotic songs like *Sommermädchenküssetauschelächelbeiche* ("Confessions of Girl's Summertime Loves and Kisses") by Gumppenberg.

Frank Wedekind

Benjamin Franklin Wedekind (1864–1918) was already a controversial writer and performer when the Eleven Executioners opened in 1901 (see Figure 3). He had self-published his first play in 1891, titled *Frühlings Erwachen* (*Spring's Awakening*). Its depictions of abortion, prostitution,

Figure 3 *Frank Wedekind, ca. 1905. ©Fine Art Images/Heritage Images/Alamy Stock Photo.*

and masturbation among school adolescents were so shocking
that police authorities in all German-language jurisdictions
considered it pornographic. Its publication and distribution
remained legal, but no producer would go near it until
1905, when Max Reinhardt produced a severely amended
version in Berlin. Most also considered Wedekind himself a
troublemaker. He had fathered an illegitimate child by actress
Frida Strindberg (who had recently divorced the Swedish
playwright August Strindberg), which to many observers
in Munich was likewise shocking. Munich police officials
found his American citizenship somewhat suspicious and
Wedekind had become the subject of several investigations.
He had been born in Hannover, but he was conceived in
San Francisco. He had grown up in Switzerland, where his
father had bought a castle in Lenzburg and insisted that his
son make his nationality a matter of personal choice. When
young Franklin learned that his father's will left him a small
bequest of 20,000 gold Swiss francs, he headed for Paris—but
not to become a French citizen. In the French capital he found
innumerable "gaslights, horse-drawn omnibuses, cabarets,
and demonstrating feminists" (Shattuck 1969: 16). His stated
goal in Paris, he said, was to have as much sex as he could
afford and then write ballads, songs, and plays about his
experiences (Kutscher 1927: 262). Those experiences included
visits not only to brothels, but also to several circuses, café-
concerts, and cabarets. They also included the acquaintance
of Albert Langen (1869–1909), who had established himself
as a successful publisher in Munich by 1890. He had seventy-
eight authors under contract, including Ibsen and Knut
Hamsun, but he also had an inherited personal fortune. He
published Wedekind's first "Lulu" play, titled *Erdgeist* (Earth
Spirit) and, like Wedekind, attended cabaret performances
in Montmartre. But unlike Wedekind Langen had come
to Paris looking for writers of talent whose work he might
publish in German. In the process he discovered the numerous
broadsheet publications and illustrated weeklies the cabarets
published, such as Bruant's *Le Mirliton* and Salis' *Chat Noir*.

Langen's encounter with them prompted him to inaugurate the illustrated satirical weekly *Simplicissimus* when he returned to Munich. Wedekind discovered, on the other hand, particularly in the work of Aristide Bruant, that personality could be the basis of cabaret performance, along with an interest in prostitution and songs about street life. Wedekind also became aware of the enormous sums Bruant was earning, as both a performer and a music publisher.

Langen returned to Munich in 1896. Wedekind returned later, after spending some time in London, savoring that city's practitioners of prostitution and its circuses. Langen then began publishing the aforementioned *Simplicissimus*, which he hoped would lend publicity to a new division within his publishing empire devoted to contemporary art, drama, and literature. Langen wanted to bring the Parisian graphic artist Theophile-Alexandre Steinlen to Munich, but their negotiations fell apart when Steinlen could not get out of his numerous contracts in Paris. From Steinlen, Langen learned the importance of an easily recognized publishing emblem, such as the black cat which Steinlen had created for Rudolphe Salis.

Simplicissimus soon gained a wide readership. It represented everything that liberal Germans hated about Wilhelminian taste and politics: prudery, philistinism, militarism, imperialism, patriotism, hero worship, inherited privilege, religious orthodoxy, and authoritarian law enforcement. *Simplicissimus* was one of the first weeklies to gain a readership outside of German-speaking Europe. Its frequent contributors included not only Wedekind but also Ludwig Thoma, Roda Roda, Kurt Tucholsky, Christian Morgenstern, Korfitz Holm, Hermann Bahr, Max Halbe, the aforementioned Ernst von Wolzogen and Julius Otto Bierbaum, along with several other liberals whom we today might describe as "anti-Establishment types." *Simplicissimus* also published French lyrics, ballads, interviews, and short stories which Langen and Countess Franziska "Fanny" zu Reventlow (1871–1918) translated into German. The first issue, published in April 1896, featured work by twenty-four different authors.

In 1899, Langen published a poem by Wedekind in *Simplicissimus* titled "In the Holy Land." It was a spoof on the visit of Kaiser Wilhelm II to Jerusalem in 1898, and it earned Wedekind and the illustrator Heine five-month prison terms, while the authorities slapped a heavy fine on Langen. Nonetheless, Wedekind's arrest and imprisonment created such a sensation that sales of the journal ran to over 100,000 copies. Thereafter, subscriptions and individual sales exceeded 85,000 per week, which brought Langen a sizeable income. Meanwhile Wedekind, having been imprisoned, needed money. Although he had initially rejected the idea of performing in cabaret, he saw that the cabaret mania could offer him a more or less regular income in Munich, while advertising both himself and his literary works.

In his first appearance at the Eleven Executioners after his release from prison, he sang his "Maulkorb" (Dog's Muzzle) to the tune of the German national anthem ("Deutschland, Deutschland, über Alles") "Gag and muzzle, most important! Make it fit right over the snout. Not a single word discordant, then you're free as sauerkraut! But believe me when I tell you: this is not a Prussian joke! Nor, you ox-head, to repel you from that gorgeous German yoke." He also included in his act (accompanying himself on the lute) "Der Tantenmörder" (The Aunt Killer), which, unlike any of the "death ballads" of Bruant, was actually very funny aside from the homicidal sentiments:

> I just murdered my aunt but the lady was old and was weak. I had spent the night at her place, so I rifled her jewel box, so to speak. / I found there a glistening treasure / Full of bills and money galore / But I felt no love nor compassion / When the old bag started to snore. / No need for pity or sorrow / So I stuck my knife deep into her guts / And she won't be snoring tomorrow.

As the applause rang through the place, he stood stock still, acknowledging nothing and no one. The same was true when audiences booed him. Yet Wedekind enjoyed performing and was apparently highly effective. "As the Marquis of Keith in the play of the same title, he left the professionals in the shade," Brecht said.

> As a singer, he had a brittle voice, a kind of untaught monotone. But no singer has ever filled me with such delight and shock. He was so filled with energy and vitality that he was able to overwhelm both applause and scorn ... He seemed immortal somehow, like Tolstoy and Strindberg, two of the great teachers of the new Europe. His greatest work was his personality.
>
> (Brecht 1957: 3–4)

Wedekind opened with the Eleven Executioners in April 1901, the only member of the troupe who eschewed a pseudonym. All the other Executioners had assumed names for themselves (such as "Max Knax," "Balthasar Starr," or "Dionysius Tod"). Wedekind was more concerned, as Mary Paddock has noted, with his public image. He wanted German audiences to take him seriously, both personally and professionally. "Why a pseudonym?" Wedekind asked fellow Executioner Otto Falckenberg. "If you're on the stage, there you are. There's no hiding it" (Falckenberg 1944: 166). Wedekind exploited his infamy, coming on to young girls with obscene suggestions about their pretended virginity or other aspects of their persons. Brecht loved Wedekind's act, which "filled every corner of the stage with his own personality. He stood there, ugly, close-cropped copper-colored red hair, brutal, dangerous, hands in his pants pockets" (Brecht 1957: 3).

Kathi Kobus

Wedekind also performed at a Munich "literary tavern" called *Simplicissimus*. The place was the creation of Katharina "Kathi" Kobus (1854–1929), who began life as a Bavarian peasant in Taunstein, a small town near the Austrian border.

When she became pregnant at age seventeen, her father threw her out of the family home in disgrace. She made her way to Munich, where she presumably gave birth to the baby and worked as a waitress and artist's model for the next twenty years. By the time she was forty, she became well known as a singer in bars and taverns. In the late 1890s she was working at a wine pub and restaurant called *Dichtelei*, and there she became somewhat independent by running the place for the owner. With the backing of Slovenian painter Anton Ažbe (1862–1905), who ran an art school in the Schwabing district, she leased a tavern in the Türken Strasse in 1903. She gave it the title *Simplicissimus*, hoping to capitalize on the *éclat* accorded Langen's satirical journal of the same name.

Kobus usually kept her place open until 3:00 a.m. The front part of the venue was open to customers off the street, and the decorations were no different from those found in other such establishments: a bar where customers ordered drinks and tables with chairs where customers imbibed their beverages of choice. Through a narrow passageway, called the "intestine," customers could enter the cabaret, which had a small raised stage, a piano, and a bar. Nights when the place was crowded, people had to stand in line to make their way through the "intestine." The waiters had a difficult time managing orders and became known for their acrobatic skills in juggling glasses, bottles, and trays through the cramped opening.

The *Simplicissimus* soon became a *Künstlerkneipe* (artists' pub) where several writers and poets presented their material in exchange for free beer. Among the most significant of them were Wedekind and the humorist Joachim Ringelnatz (1883–1934), whose hilarious poetry became such an attraction that Kobus hired him as her "house poet," although the honor came with no financial recompense. The place became known to *cognoscenti* as *Simpl*, and like Wolzogen's efforts, it attracted opponents of Wilhelmine prudery and philistinism. Similar to Rudolphe Salis' first *Chat Noir*, the *Simpl*'s two rooms featured paintings and drawings of artists who used the place as a free gallery. None of the performers were paid; Kobus kept a close check on accounts and only sometimes "paid" performers with drinks or wall space for their artwork. She appeared most often in her Bavarian dirndl dress, playing the "tough hostess" and never letting things get out of hand. One exception was the night when Isadora Duncan supposedly danced nude for hours on the stage, the tables, and any other space available, much to the roaring approval and amusement of customers.

Sometimes brawls broke out, and Kobus plunged into the fracas to restore order. She might physically throw out unruly patrons. One night the Kaiser's son Crown Prince Wilhelm (1882–1951) showed up incognito with one of his boyfriends, and they became both noisy and demanding. Kobus called out, "Shut up, you Prussian pigs!" and they dutifully obeyed her. Today Kobus is remembered in glossaries and lexicons as an "artistic hostess" but her venue was a cabaret in everything but name: like that of Salis in Montmartre it was small, the artists performed or displayed their own work, and audience participation was a nightly event. *Simpl* attracted writers and other members of the bohemian crowd who had patronized the Executioners. Eric Mühsam and Detlev von Liliencron read their satirical poetry aloud. Wedekind sang his whore songs and played guitar, and all of the former Executioners were steady customers. Emmy Hennings sang on a regular basis and met Hugo Ball there, an encounter which proved to be fateful for the history of cabaret, as we shall see. There was no one to replace Marc Henry as master of ceremonies, who at the time was on tour with Marya Delvard, but Mühsam became adept at the *Simpl* for a style of verse called *Schüttelreim*. It interchanged the consonants of some words, creating humorous if sometimes bizarre meanings. In German one example is *Liegt der Bauer auf der Lauer, dann auf der Dauer wird ihr Mann ganz sauer*. In translation, its humor is mostly lost: "If the farmer makes a habit of sleeping with Frau Lauer, then her husband will start to get real sour." A good example in English is calling farmers "tons of soil" instead of "sons of toil." Another might be "One farmer raised gourmet produce, but the other's produce was more gay, we may adduce."

Ringelnatz became the best known of the humorous poets at the *Simpl*. He had been expelled from several schools as a youth, but four years in the German merchant marine and one year in the Kaiser's Imperial Navy had a temporary maturing effect on him. He began working as an office clerk in Leipzig, but after three years he left Leipzig and tried to support himself as a singer of his own compositions. He ended up in several flophouses and jails, but by 1909 he had once again returned to steady work in a Munich bookstore. In that year he discovered the *Simpl* and began presenting his songs and poetry there. As Kathi Kobus' "house poet" the two had a remarkable relationship, perhaps because she was twenty-nine years his senior, but also because she feared that his somewhat suspicious poetry might bring the police censor down on her. Just the opposite happened, as Ringelnatz became the venue's biggest drawing card by 1913.

In that year, Kobus decided to retire. She sold the *Simplicissimus* for what was rumored to have been an extravagant sum and bought a tavern in the Bavarian Alps for RM 25,000.

Vienna

In the spring of 1901, Felix Salten opened the *Jung-Wiener Theater zum lieben Augustin* (Young Vienna Theatre St. Augustine), based on what he had seen in Berlin. Given the "cabaret epidemic" taking place there and in Munich, Salten convinced members of the informal aggregation known as "Young Vienna" to lease space in one of the city's leading playhouses, hoping to bring Vienna "up-to-date" with the latest trends in live performance and perhaps to make some money while doing so.

Vienna was the historical capital of the Habsburg Empire and since 1867 (at the conclusion of the Austro-Prussian War) the capital, along with Budapest, of the Dual Monarchy of

Austria-Hungary. It had been a cultural capital of German-speaking Europe during most of the nineteenth century. As well as its musical heritage it attracted acting, design, and playwriting talent from all over the Dual Monarchy's enormous expanse of territory. Many of the artistic talents who worked in Vienna found comfortable opportunities for the "bohemian lifestyle" discussed in the previous chapter. Vienna thus must have seemed a natural place to start on cabaret. But the first attempt to found one in Vienna was a flop.

Felix Salten (1869–1945) was born in Budapest, but his family moved to Vienna soon after he was born because the city had granted Jews full civil rights in 1867. His father went bankrupt in 1885, and the young Felix had to quit school and go to work. His first job involved clerking for an insurance company, but by 1886 he was successfully writing theater reviews for the *Austrian Art Chronicle* and then became a full-time entertainment editor for the weekly magazine *On the Blue Danube*. By1900 he was in demand as an essayist and reviewer for most of the important German-language papers in Europe. He also had an interest in "bohemianism," especially that side of bohemian life which also stimulated Bruant and Wolzogen's major obsessions: the behavior of women. He wrote many short stories about prostitutes, and one of his anonymous novels became a huge best-seller (over 3 million copies sold), titled *Josefine Mutzenbacher, oder die Geschichte einer Wienerischen Dirne von ihr selbst erzählt* (Josephine Mutzenbacher, or "The Story of a Viennese Whore, told by Herself"). His biggest hit came much later: an anthropomorphic coming-of-age story titled "Bambi," about an orphaned fawn who grows into a monumental stag with the help of other forest creatures. The story contains abundant social criticism, but the American animator and film producer Walt Disney (1901–66) largely ignored it when he used "Bambi" as the basis for his enormously popular 1942 animated film of the same title.

Salten's attempt at cabaret was the product of the Jung Wien (Young Vienna) group, who were mostly writers organized

around playwrights Hermann Bahr (1863–1934), Arthur
Schnitzler (1862–1931), Hugo von Hoffmansthal (1874–
1924), and Peter Altenberg (1859–1919). They staged their
programs in the nearly empty Theater an der Wien, a musical
house with a capacity of 1,100 seats. Frank Wedekind was a
featured performer: Salten hoped his presence would attract
enough attention to the undertaking to allow it a lengthy run.
He was disappointed in that hope, because the Viennese did
not find Wedekind's material interesting and they did not like
his singing. He sang his most popular songs ("Ilse," "Brigitte
B.," and "Die Sieben Heller") but the effect was lachrymose
(*weinerlich*), complained one critic, and another wrote that the
impression Wedekind left was one of impertinence (*Zumutung*).
Salten and his group dramatized ballads sung by Viennese
operetta performers, but the response was likewise negative.
Young Vienna Theatre St. Augustine ceased operations after
five performances.

Vienna waited five years for another cabaret to form, and
the individuals who did it were none other than the Frenchman
Marc Henry and his girlfriend Marya Delvard. When the Eleven
Executioners went out of business in 1904, Henry and Delvard
went on tour with some members of the group. It proved to
be handsomely profitable, with engagements in Bavaria,
then into Austria at Graz, then to western Bohemia. It was
good to have a French master of ceremonies in Bohemia, one
member of the group said, because anti-German feeling was
strong among the Czechs. They then toured Prussia, hoping
to capitalize on the popularity of cabaret in Berlin. They were
not disappointed, but in the northern cities along the Baltic
and North Sea coasts, houses were half-empty and audience
response was lukewarm. Even Hamburg was disappointing.

In 1905, Delvard accepted an engagement at the Apollo
Theatre, a well-known and popular *Varieté* venue in Vienna. At
the conclusion of her engagement at the Apollo, she and Henry
opened the Modernes Cabaret in the Führrich Gasse. Their lease
ran out after two months, so in the spring of 1906 they made
another attempt, this time with the help of some influential

Viennese writers and publishers, to create a literary cabaret called *Nachtlicht* (Night Light). Henry convinced composer and former Executioner Hannes Ruch to join them, and later so did the Danish-American singer and dancer Gertrude Barrison. Henry reached his peak in Vienna, developing the master of ceremonies as a figure who held the entire show together from beginning to end, and with commentary between the acts. His was not an act like the others. He had served as master of ceremonies at the Eleven Executioners, but he was listed as one of the group. In Vienna, however, he created the impression that the proceedings were his creation.

A distinctive feature of the Night Light cabaret was the work of Peter Altenberg, Roda Roda, Felix Dörmann, and Karl Kraus, who presented their own material in between the songs of Delvard and the humorous observations of Henry. There was even an attempt to present a one-act play, which Kraus directed. But Kraus grew tired of what he termed the "artistic megalomania" on display at the Night Light, and he singled out Delvard in one widely published denunciation. One evening after a performance, Henry found Kraus in the Casino de Paris restaurant in Vienna. He demanded an apology, insulting Kraus as "a common Jew," and called for waiters to throw him out. They did Henry's bidding twice until after Kraus' third reappearance. Henry began to beat Kraus mercilessly until he fell unconscious to the floor. Delvard then started kicking the unconscious Kraus, as the two waiters who had twice escorted Kraus from the premises now laid him out on a restaurant table. Vienna police later cited Henry on criminal charges, and a court sentenced him to a month in jail. The same court then levied a fine of 300 Kroner against Delvard (Shaw 1989: 193).

The Night Light closed in December 1906, but in January of the following year came a stupendous offer to Henry and Delvard from Fritz Wärndorfer (1868–1939). Wärndorfer was heir to an industrial cotton-processing concern, the largest such corporation in the Austro-Hungarian Empire, and by 1907 was one of the major sponsors of the Wiener-Werkstätten

movement. The Werkstatt (Workshop) movement in Vienna
had begun in 1903, envisioning itself as the Continental
continuation of the British Arts and Crafts Movement, founded
in 1893. The Arts and Crafts Movement was an attempt to
put the concepts of John Ruskin into practice, emphasizing
traditional craftsmanship, a rejuvenation of decorative
arts, and the embrace of the *art nouveau* style in "applied
arts." In the German language, that style became *Jugendstil*
("Youthful Style)," which emphasized aesthetically pleasing
practical objects (such as chairs, lampshades, and a host of
other applications). In many ways, the "applied arts" idea and
Bierbaum's idea of "applied lyrics" for cabaret accorded with
one another.

Wärndörfer moved the group into a splendid, newly re-
novated venue in Kärntner Strasse. Architect Josef Hoffmann
designed the interior as a *Jugendstil* showpiece, and indeed the
interior was one of the venue's main attractions. The enterprise
was a singular occasion for the Vienna Art Nouveau movement
and the Vienna Secession[5] movement to collaborate. Hoffmann
recruited Gustav Klimt, Oskar Kokoschka, Koloman Moser,
Carl Leopold Hollitzer, and Emil Orlik to decorate the
cabaret's interior, and those artists were also responsible for
the cabaret's programs along with its advertising posters.
Everything connected with the *Fledermaus* emanated taste,
high culture, modernist form—in other words, the Vienna
Secession movement. A few days prior to opening before an
invited audience, each member of the audience received an
elegant packet of materials explaining Wärndorfer's approach,
including a sixteen-page program on glossy paper with
embossed headers which introduced individuals associated
with the project. The gilt-edged program grandiloquently
proclaimed that *Die Fledermaus* was intended to become a
different kind of cabaret, one that integrated high-minded
artistry with refined cultural taste. The founders were mindful
of including all the arts in an effort to satisfy discriminating
palates within the audience. To that end, there was a
commitment to an intimate audience–performer relationship,

so that the viewer will have a feeling of experiencing artistic life on stage. But by no means, the program insisted, was there to be any sense of "naturalistic illusion." The goal was to stimulate an ambience, not simulate reality. The eyes of the audience were to feast on the play of colors and light, but the place eschewed "fake gaudiness." Wärndorfer's chief aim was to stimulate the audience's imagination within an aesthetically confined space, where the founders lavished details on lighting fixtures, tablecloths, eating utensils, tableware, and even the doorknobs, attested to a unified basic theme: "A site that serves the culture of entertainment."

Wärndorfer spared no expense for the opening festivities, including a chef from Paris, whiskey from the United States, and a chamber orchestra made up of instrumentalists from the Vienna Symphony who played out of sight, under the stage. There were no reserved seats, and patrons were encouraged to eat and drink while enjoying the performances taking place. Guests included aristocrats, millionaires, well-connected artists, financiers, scientists, and well-known courtesans who accompanied rich young men. Marya Delvard soon became the star attraction of the Fledermaus. But in this venue she eschewed traditional cabaret songs whose themes were about suffering, decadence, whoring, and crime. They instead emphasized frivolity, pseudo-naiveté, and the ironic.

3

Offshoots: Prague, Krakow, Budapest, Moscow, Zurich

Prague

The term "cabaret" appeared in Prague for the first time when the Commerce and Trade Association produced small-stage performances as part of its exhibition at the Prague Exhibition Grounds in 1908. The exhibition's organizers had hired Jaroslav Kvapil (1868–1950), who at the time was director of the Národní Divadlo (National Theatre), to organize a performance ensemble to entertain visitors at the exhibition. At the time, Kvapil was best known as the librettist for composer Antonin Dvorak's 1901 opera *Rusalka*. He had seen professional cabaret troupes in Berlin and Vienna, and he hired individuals who, he believed, could effectively copy what was taking place in Germany and Austria. Prague at the time was partly German-speaking, an important urban center in the Austro-Hungarian Dual Monarchy. The program Kvapil organized was so popular at the exhibition that some of the performers decided to create a full-time troupe to entertain at restaurants and taverns in the city. The cabaret troupe's leading personality was Karel Hašler (1879–1941),

who had already embarked on a career as a comedian and
musical performer under Kvapil at the National Theatre. By
1910, Hašler had established the troupe in a small space at the
ornate Lucerna Palace in Wenceslas Square. It was an excellent
location, because Wenceslas Square was (and still is) one of
the city's major gathering places; it is a major boulevard in
the city, rather than an intersection of thoroughfares. It thus
resembled the Champs Élysées in Paris or Unter den Linden in
Berlin. At the Commerce and Trade exhibition, Hašler worked
as the master of ceremonies, though he also sang and appeared
in brief comic sketches.

Attorney Jiří Červený (1887–1962) with several friends
founded the *Červená sedma* (Seven of Hearts) cabaret in late
1909. Though he was not a professional performer by any
means, Cerveny became the group's master of ceremonies.
He soon became adept at presenting a kind "talked-through"
song, and with his Seven of Hearts colleagues wrote what some
believe to have been over 400 such songs, of which only about
thirty have survived. The Seven of Hearts experienced a major
improvement with the 1913 arrival of satirist and poet Eduard
Bass (1888–1946) in their midst. Bass was a professional
satirist, having published several articles in popular magazines.
He had often visited Munich, and he had lived there from 1905
to 1906. There he witnessed the *Simplicissimus* venue and
some offshoots of the Eleven Executioners, but his day job as
a representative of his father's brush manufacturing company
prevented him from much participation in any cabaret work.
His endeavors with the Seven of Hearts were not great literary
efforts, but they were humorous enough to attract a wide
following to the new venue the group occupied in Hybernska
Street at the Central Hotel, near the central train station in
Prague. Bass also played piano with the group, and he was one
of the rare Czech cabaret entertainers who could do an effective
comedy routine while accompanying himself on the keyboard.

A cabaret called Montmartre was one of Prague's noteworthy
venues with literary aspirations. Its leading personality Josef

Waltner had leased space in a large old building named *U třech divých* ("the House at the Three Savages"), and its idioms of performance marked its departure from the strategies of other Prague cabarets. The music, sketches, dance numbers, poetry readings, and Waltner's routines as master of ceremonies were not only in Czech but also in German and Yiddish. Waltner liked a kind of "free-form" format, which allowed him at times to perform also as a dancer. There was also ragtime music from New Orleans, along with tangos from Buenos Aires and apache dance numbers similar to those in Paris. The venue's interior was distinctive as well: it featured Cubist paintings, imaginative frescoes, and graphics by well-known Prague artists, and its regular customers included the likes of Jaroslav Hašek, Egon Erwin Kisch, Max Brod, and Franz Kafka.

Kafka's nights at the Montmartre were indicative of a growing interest among Europeans for African-inflected music. Kafka and his friends frequented not only Montmartre but also other night haunts that offered ragtime and Africanized, "proto-jazz" entertainments. Proprietor Waltner also presented dancers who specialized in the "cakewalk" and other promenade-style strutting. The weirdest embodiment of "proto-jazz" in Prague cabarets was perhaps best manifested at a cabaret called *Konvikt* (Jailbird) where a "jazz machine" made its debut. The machine was a kind of player piano encompassed by various percussion instruments such as bells, hollow tubes, cymbals, gongs, drums, and loaded shotgun barrels. The player could trigger the shotgun at particularly loaded moments in the music with specially outfitted foot pedals.[1] The principal feature of the machine was its ability to produce syncopated rhythms, which at the time contributed to what some critics called simply "black noise" or what Thompson calls "jazzed atonality." Like cabaret in general, it represented an "ambiguous cultural hybrid, intellectualized and then ironized to the point of becoming highly influential aesthetic practices" (Thompson 2016: 70).

Krakow

The center of Polish cabaret interest was located in Krakow, perhaps because it was (like Prague) under Austrian suzerainty; cultural winds blowing in from Western Europe and the United States often swept into what is now western Poland. At the turn of the nineteenth century, when the cabaret epidemic was gathering steam, there was no Poland. There was likewise no Czech Republic. Yet historians often refer to the years between 1890 and 1914 with the term *Młoda Polska* ("Young Poland") to denote a growing sense of Polish nationalism, especially among relatively young Polish intellectuals. Like their counterparts in the "Young Vienna" movement, few of them were actually young. Yet their political opinions, their nationalistic convictions, and their aesthetic principles found a surprising resonance among Polish intellectuals and elites. They wanted to bring Poland, its language, and its performance culture "up-to-date" with the latest trends in Paris and Berlin.

Most of the movement's adherents lived in Krakow, the ancient capital of Poland and the seat of its best university. Among the movement's most vocal advocates were poet Antoni Lange (1863–1929), who had been expelled from the University of Warsaw for his nationalistic utterances, and critic Zenon Przesmycki (1861–1944) who used the pen name "Miriam." Miriam was particularly antagonistic toward cabaret, and his denunciations reflect a kind of split among intellectuals as to how Polish nationalism should best manifest itself. He stated that any attempt to "transplant" onto Polish soil "the most wretched, most insipid, and most speculative of German products, namely 'cabaret,'" was doomed to failure. The Germans themselves, he noted, "have realized the worthlessness of cabaret. Cabaret is by no means a worthwhile development in terms of literature nor in the evolution of culture. Other Germans have denounced cabaret as a detestable misuse of art's holy name" (in Segal 1987: 232).

Among other concerns that exercised Polish intellectuals was a tendency to emulate Western European cultural trends, which resulted in a persistent apathy among Poles to agitate for an independent, non-partitioned Poland. Other Polish intellectuals, unlike Miriam, particularly after the 1905 Russian Revolution, began to conceive of cabaret as a vehicle for loosening censorship. Thus in October 1905, the Green Balloon (*Zielony Balonik*) cabaret opened its doors in Krakow. It was the brainchild of dramatist Jan August Kisielewski (1876–1918), who had recently returned from a lengthy sojourn to Paris. There he had spent considerable time in Montmartre, attending performances at the *Chat Noir* and *Le Mirliton*. His experiences there persuaded him that Krakow was ready to accept an attempt to imitate what he had seen in Montmartre. In his view, cabaret represented a much hoped-for window of opportunity for Polish intellectuals, perhaps even a public platform to present their ideas about, their hopes for, and their dreams of a united Poland. The Green Balloon opened in 1905 in Cukierna Lwowska (The Lvov Confectionary), a kind of restaurant-patisserie, where it remained for the next seven years. His friend and fellow Young Poland devotee Tadeusz Boy-Zelenski (1874–1941), who had recently married a close protégé of Young Poland playwright Stanislav Wyspianski, agreed to serve as the group's organizational leader. Like Bruant, Wolzogen, Bierbaum, and Wedekind, Boy-Zelenski combined literary and political enthusiasm with an interest in women. His interests, however, were clinical rather than erotic. He was a trained gynecologist, and in the late 1890s he had built a successful medical practice. By 1906, his reputation in gynecology was so lucrative that he gained the financial freedom to pursue his interest in performing.

The Green Balloon attracted several writers who had political viewpoints at odds with the authorities. Boy-Zelenski spread rumors via anonymous letters to newspapers that the cabaret was actually a cover for all-night dancing and drunken orgies in the darker corners of the pastry restaurant. Although police authorities discovered no raucous or indecent behavior, the ploy of using rumor to attract business succeeded flawlessly. There were so many would-be patrons wanting admission to the Green Balloon on most nights that Boy-Zelenski had the luxury of exercising caution in the admission process. He actively discriminated among individuals desirous of tickets, because he wanted an elite audience, such as professors at the Krakow Academy of Fine Arts, artists and their friends, theater people, journalists, and enthusiastic visitors from Warsaw. Sometimes Boy-Zelinski even included government officials, who sang and performed. He apparently also agreed to accommodate police spies because he knew many of them, but his preference remained for well-established bourgeois sophisticates. The venue was well-appointed with green velvet upholstery—it was, after all, one of Krakow's fanciest patisseries, but the entire place could accommodate only about 100 patrons. People came there well-dressed and in a mood to enjoy themselves—even if it meant being insulted by Jan August Kisielewski before the show got started.

Kisielewski greeted audiences at the Green Balloon in the style of Bruant, insulting everybody and insisting that they sit close together. Then he turned his specific attention to "pseudo-sophisticates," whom he termed "hieroglyphs of ignorance" who, in imitation of their Viennese counterparts, "decked themselves out in the feathers of a dead peacock." Such "syphilids," he said, were holding back the progress of Polish culture. They were guilty of "simian maliciousness, a dwarf's impertinence, street sentimentality, tobacco-shop aestheticism, and parochial pretentiousness" (Segal 1987: 230). They loved it. The space was intimate, similar in many ways to the Fledermaus in Vienna. There was a small podium near the piano. Most nights the place was filled to capacity and its prosperity led the owner of the pastry shop to add a second room to allow for additional seating.

Boy-Zelinski eventually became a superb master of ceremonies, replacing Kisielewski after a few months. Unknown to most of his friends, he had long been a student of the French chanson, a result of his extensive translation work: by 1914 he had translated the entire works of Moliére into Polish. Later, he translated works by Balzac, Rousseau, Marivaux, and Descartes. He also filled the role of a Young Poland crusader, especially when it came to women. His mission, many believed, was to remove the Polish veil that had historically covered the subject of eroticism. To him, that veil was nothing more than prudery. He brought his gynecologist's training and practice into the struggle by discussing sexuality in biological and physiological terms. In 1906, he published a remarkable poem titled "An Open Letter from a Polish Woman," in which a woman does nothing but wait for someone who will finally take off her halo of holiness and remove from her the shallow mask of chastity. In another poem titled "The Reply of a Woman," a writer expresses dissent against the image of a Polish woman that appears in the works of several Polish poets. There, the dissenter claims, poets had depicted woman "without lingerie / As the symbol of the Homeland. / Her bed was the sacrificial stake!"

The Green Balloon's success stimulated Krakow native Arnold Syfman (1882–1967) to open the *Momus* cabaret in Warsaw in 1908. That venue is perhaps most notable for its status as a profit-oriented enterprise that sold admission tickets to its presentations. It represented a new type of middlebrow entertainment available to Warsaw residents, who formed an audience that expected to see a well-prepared performance for its money. The texts were written mostly by ambitious playwrights, along with the talents of Mary Morozinska, who some claimed was the "Polish Yvette Guilbert."

Budapest

The cabaret contagion reached Budapest likewise by the early 1900s. Budapest already had dozens of cafés, small music halls, and bars that offered entertainment, but all of the performers were amateurs. Most of the shows were furthermore in

German, because few within the Austro-Hungarian elites who
controlled the country believed the Hungarian language could
compete with German as a performance idiom, especially
in lowbrow sub-genres that featured or emphasized bawdy
humor. The first cabaret performance in Hungarian took place
in 1901 in Pest, the eastern component of the city, in a night
club which emulated the Colorful Theater in Berlin. It was a
small venue that eschewed ribald jokes, off-color punch lines,
and sight gags in favor of short sketches that commented on
current political trends and personalities. Performers sang
songs that were tastefully amusing, a description that also
fitted their costumes: evening gowns for ladies that revealed
nothing and tuxedos for the men that helped them maintain
their dignity.

The undertaking was a complete flop. "It was just too much
for the people," said Dezső Gyárfás (1882–1921) one of the
performers. "One or two songs in Hungarian is still OK. But
the whole evening!" (Gyárfás 1920). Most venues returned to
German-language presentations until 1907, when a Hungarian
actor named Ernő Kondor (1881–1951) invested a large and
unexpected inheritance in a new venture he called *Kabaré
Bonbonnière*. It took place in an empty shop he had rented
on Teréz körut (Therese Boulevard), a main thoroughfare
in downtown Pest; he had a stage at one end, and filled the
place with chairs and tables. It resembled similar places with
an intimate atmosphere found in Munich or Paris, but his
show differed little in format from the one that had failed so
badly in 1901. What had changed was the economic situation
in Budapest, which had provided Hungarian audiences
an unaccustomed amount of disposable income. Those
Hungarians involved in rapid industrialization, infrastructure
developments, and property businesses were now enjoying
unprecedented success; the middle-class professions did not do
as well, but they were much better off than they had been as
recently as ten years earlier. Both groups were now interested
in how *kabaré* in the Hungarian language might engage them
and their new affluence.

The cast performing at Kondor's *Kabaré Bonbonnière* were all native Hungarian speakers, and their musical choices, while familiar, contained an element of unceremoniousness to which audiences positively responded. The authors who wrote comic sketches for the group included young writers and critics whose work had manifested little previous experience of having been performed in public, such as Lajos Balint, Oskar Beregi, and Sandor Rott. The key element in the whole operation, and its acceptance among Hungarian audiences, was Endre Nagy (1877–1938). Like his Polish contemporary Tadeusz Boy-Zelenski, Nagy discovered that he had real talent as a master of ceremonies. Unlike Boy-Zelenski, Nagy had a serious speech impediment. Yet he incorporated his lisping and stammering into his opening monologues. His commentary between sketches or musical numbers and his improvisations on contemporary themes greatly amused his audiences. His difficulties created the impression of awkwardness and uncertainty, which many in his audience found charming.

Kondor placed Nagy in charge of *Bonbonnière*'s programs, and Nagy gradually transformed the show into a humorous "News of the Week" routine, adding songs and sketches that resembled semi-official newspaper reports. In 1908, Nagy (see Figure 4) left the *Bonbonnière* and went to work for the *Modern Cabaret* in Budapest. Nagy continued there to focus on mundane topics such as the price of coffee beans or the scarcity of whalebone for ladies' corsets, "becoming a kind of Mr. Hungarian Cabaret in the process of caricaturing Hungarian political and social absurdities" (Prokopovych 2014: 279). One of Nagy's outstanding discoveries was Romanian-born Vilma Medgyasczay (1885–1972), who was unique among all *diseuses* in European cabarets by virtue of her chansons based on the compositions of Bela Bartok and Zoltan Karoly, two composers whose modernist dissonances remained unheard and unknown to most cabaret patrons. She took over the leadership of the Modern Cabaret when Nagy departed in 1913. Her style of singing was also a departure from the styles of Yvette Guilbert or Marya Delvard: it was

Figure 4 *Endre Nagy, sketch by Miklós Agassiz. Courtesy of Alamy Stock Photo.*

comparatively sentimental and even delicate, yet possessing "dramatic power." In other words, she knew what pleased Budapest audiences most: a rendering of Hungarian lyrics in what could best be described as a "folk style" (Pungur 2012: 1752). It accorded with the overall approach of Hungarian cabaret itself in the words of sketch writer and critic Dezső Kosztolányi: "Our cabaret does not evoke the fresh witticism and charming malice of watering holes in the Montmartre; it's not as bloody, deadly and nerve-racking as the Berlin cabarets and does not parade with shallow, foolish philistine frivolities like those in Vienna. From the very beginnings, the Budapest cabaret was more demanding, more glittering, and more sensitive than any other" (Kosztolányi 2009).

Moscow

Cabaret in Moscow resembled the attempts of Max Reinhardt in Berlin to create a kind of parody theater, a place where local actors (particularly from the Moscow Art Theatre) could congregate after hours and laugh at satirical impressions of themselves. The first such venue opened in March of 1908 and called itself *Lituchaya mysh* (Литучая мышь), or "the Bat." It might have been related to the Viennese cabaret likewise called the Bat (*Die Fledermaus*), but this one had no pretensions to the Art Nouveau stylings of the Vienna venue, nor did it benefit from a generous sponsor like Fritz Wärndorfer. This one aspired instead to be a kind of oasis for its members and at times a kind of studio for trying out experiments. Membership in the organization (originally about forty individuals) was restricted to actors alone, but within a few months of its founding it expanded to include painters, musicians, singers, and writers. It nevertheless bore the ponderous imprint of the Moscow Art Theatre throughout its existence, which came to an end shortly after the Russian Revolution of 1917. Its leader was a minor actor of Armenian ancestry from the Moscow Art Theatre, Nikita Baliev (1877–1936), who arranged for the group's first locale, the basement of a building on the banks of the Moscow River near the Cathedral of Christ the Savior, about two city blocks from the Kremlin.

By 1910, Baliev and the *Lituchaya mysh* group began to charge admission to their festivities, a sign of their growing popularity and a means to help them move from their original venue to larger one in the cellar of the nearby Central Telegraph Building in Moscow, further north of the river but still close to the Kremlin. Its last move came in 1913, by which time *Lituchaya mysh* was a landmark of Moscow nightlife. With public admission by then set at the exorbitant fee of 12 rubles a person, it relocated to a spacious cellar beneath Moscow's largest apartment building, just off Tverskaya Street.

In this location, *Lituchaya mysh* continued the practice of opening for business after midnight, largely because both audiences and performers arrived after performances elsewhere. Performances at the Bat were, however, vastly different in style from those realistic endeavors that had just concluded in many Moscow theaters. Baliev remained the prime mover of the undertaking, and he had assumed the role of master of ceremonies. Though he had rarely received a speaking part in Moscow Art Theatre productions, his abundant energy and distinctive stage presence (he stood slightly over five feet three inches in height, and weighed about 180 lbs) made him a natural master of ceremonies—not as svelte as Marc Henry, but equally amusing as Tadeusz Boy-Zelenski. In his function as master of ceremonies, Baliev wore formal evening wear and sported a white chrysanthemum in his lapel button hole. Stanislavski was impressed with Baliev:

> His imperturbable humor, always appropriate, and his verve had a kind of audacity that skirted the border of impertinence. He [had] a sense of artistic amplitude and a comprehension of what divides merriment and cynicism. And his blathering spiced with a shot of bonhomme—all this together made him an artistic figure of a new direction, and we beheld it right before our eyes.
>
> (Stanislavsky 1987: 439)

Freed from the constraints Stanislavski placed upon them with his approach to finding the "inner life" of the characters, many Moscow Art Theatre actors enjoyed entertaining themselves into the early hours by improvising spoofs on the plays in which they had just acted. This was very different from Max Reinhardt's initial Noise and Smoke parodies. Reinhardt and his group found the then-fashionable artistic disciplines of naturalism and symbolism somewhat ludicrous. Performers at *Lituchaya mysh* felt otherwise, and indeed Stanislavsky himself performed with them on occasion. Their targets were often their own roles, with actors caricaturing their performances. Caricature at the Bat became a kind of auto- or self-parody, rather than a parody of the plays (as was the case with Reinhardt). The Bat thus emerged as a kind of alter ego of the Moscow Art Theatre, a comic double, so to speak.

Some nights the program featured metaphorical wrestling matches, in which a stereotypical and effeminate Frenchman grappled with a burly Russian for literary supremacy. There were Punch and Judy puppet shows. Gordon Craig's elaborate production of *Hamlet* in 1912 provided "golden opportunities" for Bat satire, especially Craig's interpretation of Hamlet as a Christ-like figure. The presence of Craig's lover Isadora Duncan gave impetus to Baliev's interest in dance parodies at *Lituchaya mysh*, but even as his reputation grew as the master of ceremonies *sans pareil* and audiences clamored in greater numbers for admission tickets, the Bat kept its emphasis on intimacy of performance. Baliev nevertheless recognized the importance of increasing the size of his audience, especially an audience affluent enough to afford his high ticket prices.

A good example of the kind of sketches Baliev presented involved a scene set in France, soon after Napoleon Bonaparte (1769–1821) had proclaimed himself emperor. The scene took place in an ornate drawing room, where Napoleon is in the midst of a heavy discussion with "Empress Josephine," Napoleon's first wife. After some meaningless exchanges between them, a lieutenant appears and the Emperor inquires if the limousine is ready. The young officer is embarrassed to say that it is not, because they cannot locate the chauffeur. Napoleon then launches into the inadequacy of the court and its servants, when someone whom Baliev had planted in the audience shouted, "Nonsense! There were no automobiles in Napoleon's time!" The actor playing Napoleon attempts to carry the scene forward, but again the impertinent audience member interrupts him. Other plants in the audience tell the discontented audience member to be quiet, and an argument ensues among other audience plants. Finally, Napoleon tears the wig off his head and says he cannot continue under such conditions. Baliev reappears, apparently distraught, and tries to calm things down. As the curtain falls, he begged the audience

for understanding, and the houselights come up for the show's
intermission (Senelick 1989: 177–8). In this example we see
how cabaret's original intimacy has progressed through the
phase of insulting the audience from the stage through to
locating the main interest of the sketch off-stage, among the
"audience" itself.

Zurich

The relative autonomy of Zurich from 1915 to 1917 allowed
several emigrés to take up residence in the city. The Russian
revolutionary Vladimir I. Ulyanov (1870–1924), known as
"Lenin," was one; the Polish revolutionary Karl Radek (1885–
1939) and the Polish painter and graphic artist Marcel Słodki
were others. So were the French-German Hans Arp (1886–
1966); the Romanians Tristan Tzara (1896–1963) and Marcel
Janco (1895–1984); and the Germans Richard Huelsenbeck
(1892–1974), Emmy Hennings (1885–1948), and Hugo Ball
(1886–1927). They were all revolutionaries of a sort, though
their efforts were most significant in the founding of the
Cabaret Voltaire in 1916. While many scholars and critics
have described their cabaret activities as precedent-setting,
others have emphasized the nihilistic, humorous, anarchistic,
or politically motivated nature of their undertaking. They
themselves described what they did as "dada."

Hugo Ball volunteered for German military service at age
twenty-eight in August 1914 but after six months' service was
discharged. The short duration of his service in uniform, he
said, allowed him to have seen enough battle on the Western
Front to make him a confirmed pacifist. The wholesale
slaughter he had witnessed convinced him that "the Devil's
own machinery had been set loose on the world" (Ball 1927:
11). The year previous, Ball had met singer Emmy Hennings
(1885–1948) at the Simplicissimus Cabaret in Munich, where
she was performing. They agreed to meet in Berlin upon

Figure 5 *Emmy Hennings. ©Nationlbibliothek, Schweizerisches Literaturarchiv, Berne/Alamy Stock Photo.*

his discharge, and from there they traveled to Zurich. They entered the city with forged papers and assumed names. Swiss authorities eventually apprehended and briefly jailed them, but a Zurich court awarded them temporary residency permits. Those permits, however, allowed them to work only part time. Ball got a job as a part-time pianist for a vaudeville troupe called "Flamingo"; he also played piano at several hotels and bars, while Hennings (see Figure 5) worked as a waitress.

In his off hours, Ball gave much thought to the idea of opening a cabaret like the ones he had seen in Berlin and Munich. In contrast to them, however, Ball's intentions were far more political, largely because of his experiences in the German military. He wanted to create an outpost of protest against German war enthusiasm, but he also wanted a kind of creative stronghold against conventional art. To do that, he said, he wanted to create a gathering place for the artistic and intellectual emigrés in Zurich. He thus proposed the idea to Dutch emigré Jan Ephraim, who was the proprietor of a pub called the *Holländische Meierei* ("The Dutch Works"). Nobody had any money to refurbish the place, and besides that, the Dutch Works already had a small stage, piano, and tables to accommodate about fifty people. Ball liked the name "Voltaire" for the cabaret, supposedly because he admired Voltaire's eighteenth-century nonconformity which had often landed him in jail or exile. There was no mention of something called "dadaism" in Ball's early cogitations, nor in the public announcements about the opening of a new cabaret in Zurich, but it turned out that there was no need for advance publicity.

The venue was packed on opening night (February 5, 1916), and during the chaos that ensued when nobody could find a seat, "four little men wearing monocles" arrived carrying portfolios under their arms and repeatedly bowed to Ball, Hennings, and others. They introduced themselves as Romanians, among them Tristan Tzara and Marcel Janco. During the proceedings, Ball read poems by Wasily Kandinsky, Elsa Lasker-Schüler, and Frank Wedekind. Hennings did renditions of songs by Bruant, Wedekind, and Eric Mühsam. One of the more noteworthy poetry readers at the cabaret's opening was Romanian emigré Samuel Rosenstock, who used the name "Tristan Tzara." He read to the audience the same poems he had read to Romanian military authorities the year previous, which convinced them that Tzara suffered from premature dementia. Tzara made no effort to convince the crowd that he was anything other than demented, and they (almost none of them Swiss) loved it. One reviewer summed up the evening in verse: "A German poet sighs in French / Romanian is spoken and sounds like Siamese / Art is in full bloom, Hallelujah. / There was even somebody from Switzerland there" (Klabund 1916). It was clear to the reviewer (Alfred Henschke, whose *nom de plume* was "Klabund") that something extraordinary had taken place, but he wasn't sure what it was.

What it was, was dadaism—"a combination," Ball said, "of buffoonery and the exaltation of a funeral mass. Every word spoken and sung here signifies a sign of disrespect for everything that demands respect in these debased times in which we live … [These times] require a respite, and our cabaret provides it" (Greul 1967: 207). In May 1916 there appeared the first dada broadsheet, the *Journal Cabaret Voltaire*, which further amplified dadaism's rejection of all social and artistic norms. There has been considerable debate since 1916 about who invented the term "dada" and what it meant. The answers are as different as the participants on opening night, nearly all of whom claimed credit in one way or another for inventing the term. It was essentially

an incarnation of the unsystematizable spirit of creativity. It was a sense of liberation through laughter. It blossomed in the Cabaret Voltaire, and bore fruit throughout Europe and America …. Their performances were marked by audience participation in protest. Its performers were provocateurs, and they aimed to surprise or shock audiences by speaking poetry or prose that was aggressively anti-logical, by experimenting with masks, costuming that

was radically anti-conventional. [Everything] was part of
the unprogrammed and chaotic attempt to liberate the
imagination from the shackles of tradition.

(Appignanesi 2004: 110–11)

"Sound" was a particular point of whimsy, especially in
Ball's approach to it. To him, journalism, party politics, and
advertising had degraded traditional European idioms and
modes of speaking beyond redemption. He sought substitutes
for language in what he termed *Lautgedichte* ("sound
poetry"), which he claimed was a peculiarly dadaist substitute
that might provide a revolutionary new performance argot
at dadaist performances. Bruant had attempted something
similar in Montmartre, but his argot, "animated, brutal,
and cynical" as it was, remained rooted in Parisian street
parlance. Ball's approach, in contrast, featured sound and
rhythm but no comprehensible words. A good example is this
brief passage from "Clouds": "*elomen elomen lefitalominai /
wolminuscaio baumnala bunga / acycam glastula feirofim
flinsi / elominiscula pluplubasch rallalaio / endremin sazassa
flumen floballala / feilobasch falljda follidi / flumbasch.*" Hugo
Ball composed six sound poems, all of which he recited in the
Cabaret Voltaire. Some scholars believe they represent the
most important contributions to the dadaist transformation of
the cabaret. Since they have seldom been reprinted, there has
been insufficient effort, some believe, to examine and analyze
them in scholarly literature.

Other scholars believe that the work of Richard Huelsenbeck
(1892–1974) in "primitive sound" and "primitivism" in
general was equally important, though somewhat more
controversial by today's standards. There was a strong dosage
of primitivism in the dadaist negation of Western civilization,
since dada represented repudiation of, or a strong destructive
urge aimed at, traditional European values. Those values they
held responsible for instigating the First World War. The war
was madness, and that madness was a product of European
certainties. Huelsenbeck in particular equated "the primitive"

with the Black African experience, but without any hint of resentment contained in later concepts of *négritude* that developed in France. Huelsenbeck wrote several *Negerlieder* (Negro Songs) and later introduced them at the Cabaret Voltaire. Audiences at the Cabaret Voltaire liked the "Negro Songs," so much that they became a regular feature of Cabaret Voltaire performance even when Huelsenbeck was not there to perform them. Huelsenbeck later stated that to enhance the authenticity of "Negro Songs," a big kettle drum should accompany recitations of them. The enthusiasm for African or African-sounding poems and others associated with the Cabaret Voltaire reflected the fascination among avant-garde groups of the late nineteenth and early twentieth centuries with the "primitive." By contrast with the "exotic" flirtation with "Africa" seen in such American composers and performers as Jelly Roll Morton and the Chocolate Kiddies, "primitivism" provided an alternative or even an antidote to corrupted Western values. The lure of what avant-garde artists regarded as pre-literate "primitive language" was closely linked to their disenchantment with traditional poetic language and their belief that the languages of their own societies had become so corrupt and degenerate that they were no longer capable of oral communication.

Regardless of his attitude or insensitivity to what was "authentic" in the primitive, Huelsenbeck was completely accurate in his estimation of what attracted the crowds to the Cabaret Voltaire: the song stylings of Emmy Hennings. She immediately became the resident chanteuse, a kind of dadaist Yvette Guilbert or Marya Delvard. Her performances garnered the largest applause, he noted, even though there is no record of the songs she sang. Huelsenbeck said she was very good at reciting Hugo Ball's poetry against war. While singing, Ball accompanied her on the piano and the audience often chimed in. She had absolutely no sense of celebrity about her. She changed costumes behind some scaffolding over which a canvas was stretched, with little guarantee of preserving her modesty. Ball's songs poked fun at everything, but they

were never insulting. Sometimes they made erotic references
to cuckolds or to brides on their wedding night, but "They
created the intimate atmosphere of the cabaret. The audience
liked listening to them, the distance between us and the enemy
grew smaller and finally everyone joined in" (Huelsenbeck
1974: 9–10).

Audiences of the Cabaret Voltaire were often poorly behaved,
and police frequently pestered proprietor Jan Ephraim about
the noise and disturbances about which neighbors complained.
Finances were also a problem, even though the crowds had
remained large and free-spending. But nobody involved with
the Cabaret Voltaire had any idea how to maintain accounts,
and the cabaret was usually late in paying its bills. On June
23, 1916, Hugo Ball collapsed after his performance. Ephraim
then shut down cabaret operations and returned to the pub
business. Cabaret Voltaire had run its brief but tumultuous
course. Dada, however, was now on the threshold of a life of
its own and dadaist performances continued on tour in various
Zurich locales for nearly a year after the Cabaret Voltaire
ceased to exist.

The Cabaret Voltaire had been located in the Spiegelgasse
area that in 1916 was full of bars and night clubs (and still
is). Jan Ephraim had a clear economic motive in having an
artists' cabaret on his premises: to attract customers in a very
competitive quarter. Ball's diaries in particular show that
they were under a lot of pressure from Ephraim to put on
something that would bring in customers and increase his sale
of alcoholic beverages. After the cabaret had shut, the events
that the dadaists put on over the next few years were in more
salubrious parts of the Zurich city center, so that the character
of the performances and of the audiences was more sedate.

As Ramsay Burt has observed, Zurich dada was essentially
a continuation of prewar avant-garde movements, all of which
shared a general impulse toward the overthrow and rejection
of established, conservative cultural traditions in an effort to
find a new utopian basis on which to rejuvenate culture. The
Zurich dadaists, however, by borrowing from African tribal

decoration, masks, drumming, and "the imagined rhythms of African poetry" were doing "roughly what the Fauves and Cubists had already attempted Paris" (Burt 1995: 67). What made dada particular and different was its specific heritage in cabaret form; thus, it consciously included a sizable admixture of laughter to what was often political and/or an expression of outrage. Entertainment, joviality, and diversion all contain a significant potential for earnings through ticket sales and/or beverage alcohol. In this respect cabaret is a precursor to what we now call "pop" culture. Like cabaret pop culture derives its impact not only from its accessibility and energy but also from its commercial appeal. Like many later celebrities right at the start cabaret performers such as Bruant, assisted by publication of sheet music, recordings of him singing and posters of him by Toulouse-Lautrec solidified his status as pop culture icon. The Cabaret Voltaire, like most of its predecessors, was also always a commercial venture.

New York

The syncopated musical styles which became popular in Europe and in some European cabarets had their origins in New Orleans, the city with the largest African American urban population in the United States until the First World War. Instrumental music in New Orleans, later called "Dixieland," was well established among "nineteenth century folk performers on banjos, fiddles, and jugs, playing small circuses, carnivals, tent shows, and medicine shows" (Hennessey 1994: 17). The ragtime style in piano prevalent in New Orleans made its appearance in published form by about 1890. In 1893, composer Scott Joplin (1868–1917) played several of his ragtime compositions at the Chicago World's Fair in 1893, and two years later his "Maple Leaf Rag" became a national sheet music hit. By 1900, several "ragtime bands" had formed in New Orleans, chief among them the ensemble of Alexander

Joseph Watzke (1872–1919). Watzke's band is thought to be the inspiration for "Alexander's Ragtime Band," which composer Irving Berlin (1888–1989) composed in 1911. The song became a massive best seller as sheet music, and later it was a hit recording for many vocalists. Dixieland music's first hit recording came in 1917, when the Victor Talking Machine Company issued a recording of the Original Dixieland "Jass" Band. This "jass" style of New Orleans instrumental music became "jazz" after the Original Dixieland recording became a noteworthy best seller, spawning several groups who imitated the style. Those groups proceeded to achieve substantial popularity in New York City dance halls and saloons.

By 1917, large segments of the African American population in the South had migrated to industrial cities of the north, most notably to Harlem, a northern district of New York's Manhattan Island (see Osofsky 1966: 128; also O'Neal 2006: 45). In Harlem, several nightspots applied the term "cabaret" to their operations, though its original usage had emerged two decades earlier in the mid-town entertainment district. The first was a small venue at West 39th Street and Broadway called the *Cabaret du Néant* in 1896; the second was the *Cabaret du Chat Noir* in 1900. Neither venue amounted to much, but in 1911 the film pioneer and Broadway producer Jesse Lasky (1880–1958) with business partner Henry B. Harris (1866–1912) built a 700-seat theater at 210 West 46th Street they called the *Folies Bergère*. There they created shows for two different sets of customers; the first gathered at 6:30 p.m. on the main floor to have dinner. They sat at small tables, with each section of tables arranged on slightly raised platforms. They had a lavish dinner, and afterwards they remained at their tables, watching a show that consisted of an elaborate display of showgirls and ballet dancers. An eighteen-year-old German-American singer/dancer named Mae (Dölger) West (1893–1980) made her Broadway debut there.

At midnight, a second show was on offer to another audience. Stagehands extended a platform level with the stage over the orchestra pit, creating a temporary stage apron that brought the performers closer to the audience. This presentation was supposedly a "cabaret show," which in fact is how Lasky billed it. It was more intimate, and the audience ate a late night supper while the performance was in progress. The presentation, while smaller and set closer to the audience, consisted of a dozen acts, and musicians were onstage with the singers and dancers. The dancers were attractive young women in "revealing attire," though there was no nudity. Lasky hired James J. Morton as "Master of Revels" for some of these performances, but it remained a vaudeville undertaking, with little of real cabaret's interaction with audience. Morton's principal job was to set up name cards for acts as they appeared and concomitantly to offer some humorous asides.[2] As Shane Vogel has determined, the term "cabaret" in New York was supposed to help "American nightlife" achieve a kind of respectability. The questionable morality of the lower classes could now be acceptably consumed under the banner of "European sophistication" (Vogel 2009: 54). Lasky's attempt to expand vaudeville into something more "European" or even "sophisticated" was in a way heroic. But it never really worked; the operation closed after six months.

In Harlem the name "cabaret" was applied to many venues which were, strictly, "nightclubs" (literally clubs that offered one-night membership to patrons). They catered exclusively to wealthy white customers, even though the proprietorship was African American and their main business was, following 1919 prohibition, the illegal purchase and consumption of alcohol.

They were legally required to call themselves cabarets, and all performers in them had to possess a "cabaret card." In 1926, the New York City Council passed a "cabaret ordinance" in an effort to control noise and commotion outside entertainment venues. But there was little to identify them as actual cabaret. There was even less attempt to present poetic expression inside them. There were no sketches that featured political commentary and scant wordplay that demonstrated a mastery of the sexual double entendre. There were instead "floor shows," which sometimes featured a dance number, but most often the dance floor was intended for use by customers. Sometimes a master of ceremonies introduced dance or musical acts, and indeed some of the musical entertainers were absolutely first rate. But at no time did the master of ceremonies make a practice of insulting his audience in the tradition of Aristide Bruant or Tadeusz Boy-Zelenski.

4

The Golden Age
of Cabaret

Escape

Berlin cabarets between the closing of Wolzogen's Überbrettl
and the outbreak of the First World War in 1914 increased in
quantity, if not quality. Peter Jelavich (1990: 101) has noted
that the first wave of German cabarets ended in numerous
closings and bankruptcies by 1903, and in their wake followed
endeavors to establish "specialty" venues called *Kneipenbrettl*
or pub cabarets. They emphasized whatever their proprietor
felt was needed to attract customers: song stylings, poetry,
humor, or even ideologies. Rarely—though with some notable
exceptions—did they feature much performing talent. Jelavich,
however, believes they succumbed to pressures from business
owners who appealed to police authorities in hopes of tightening
restrictions on the pub cabarets. Though Berlin had become
an enormously large metropolis by 1904, police authorities
tended to retain the mentality of keeping order as if they were
still serving in a Prussian army garrison town. Berlin, in fact,
had its beginnings as a garrison town. Police in the first decade
of the twentieth century continued to display a watchfulness
over non-conformist behavior with circumspection, especially

if it produced complaints about the goings-on in pub cabarets. Complaints often arrived at police offices at the instigation of variety, music hall, or vaudeville theater managers. They wanted police enforcement of the Berlin Commercial Code's Article 33, which required fire safety inspections and closing times of 11:00 p.m. Pub cabarets had been able to avoid such regulations because their shows lacked costumed performers, stage sets, or lighting.

Into this somewhat treacherous terrain strode Rudolf Nelson (1878–1960), whose musical career had begun at age five. His parents could not support their son's continued training as a classical musician, so they sent him off to work in the textile trades. He hated it, and he ultimately gained admission as a teenager to study composition at Berlin's Stern Conservatory. He soon began to hate the Stern Conservatory, too. The youthful Nelson had long since abandoned his interest in Liszt, Beethoven, and Brahms and had embraced popular music, particularly the ragtime and syncopated variety that emanated from New Orleans. He had already played in several pub-cabarets, and doing so taught him that Berlin needed a pub cabaret with idiosyncratic flair. He wanted to create a venue that had intimacy, sophistication, and a risqué stylishness: something he hoped would become *mondän*, a fashionable "hot spot" pub cabaret. The most significant acquaintance he made during his efforts as a pianist was the man who became his patron and chief financial backer: Prince Joachim Albert (1876–1939), a wealthy member of the ruling Hohernzollern dynasty and a close relative of Kaiser Wilhelm II. Joachim Albert was himself a composer of noteworthy talent and a frequent presence in Berlin pub cabarets—much to the chagrin of his family. Yet Joachim Albert's connections with Prussian high society proved beneficial for Nelson.

Joachim Albert provided a large initial financial investment in Nelson's first fashionable cabaret. It was the restaurant Roland von Berlin in the Potsdamer Strasse, a favorable location. It was also going bankrupt, and the prince's resources allowed Nelson (see Figure 6) to strike a favorable deal on

Figure 6 *Rudolf Nelson. ©Bundesnationalarchiv Berlin/Alamy Stock Photo.*

the lease and to begin extensive remodeling. The venue, when completed in 1904, accommodated about 150 patrons, seated around tables or in rows of seats. Nelson had by then hired actor and dancer Paul Schneider-Duncker (1883–1956) as master of ceremonies. Together, Nelson and Schneider-Duncker agreed on a dress code, which required everyone working at or entering their establishment to dress in "evening wear," as if they were attending an opera at the Berlin Royal Theater. Nelson's talents enabled him to imitate New Orleans musical styles—even though some "sophisticates" considered the cakewalk, ragtime, and other syncopated innovations inherently paradoxical. They believed that ladies in long ruffled frocks (and gentlemen in custom-tailored tailcoats) high-stepping through promenades and doing the cakewalk were obviously improper. Schneider-Duncker's talents as a dancer, however, resolved such contradictions. He devised innovative "moves" to Nelson's "exotic" rhythms, much to the admiration of his upscale audiences; many members of those audiences vied with each other to master the promenade-style dances coming from America, and the competition was obviously beneficial to Nelson's income accounts.

In 1907, having fallen out with Schneider-Duncker, Nelson leased another venue in the prime location of Friedrich Strasse near Unter den Linden, Imperial Berlin's high-prestige boulevard. He named it *Chat Noir* in evocation of Salis' original venue in Montmartre. Meanwhile, Schneider-Duncker had discovered the talent of a performer who had recently arrived in Berlin from Gelsenkirchen, Claire Waldoff (1884–1957). She would help Schneider-Duncker make a success of the Roland von Berlin. Working with composer Walter Kollo (1878–1940) at the piano, she premiered his "Song of the Marsh Reed" (*Schmackeduzchen-Lied*). She sang the song (about a male duck who fell in love with a marsh reed plant) in a Berlin dialect—an obvious departure from the "sophisticated" tone Nelson had presented to audiences at Roland and to which they had become accustomed. Most of Nelson's female vocalists had dressed according to the fashions he expected from female audience members, much in the way Delvard and even Emmy Hennings had appeared: corseted, coiffured, and captivating. Waldoff wore a simple dress and made no attempt to disguise her plump, somewhat thickset figure; her red hair was brushed, but it remained unruly. She wore unstylish low-cut pumps, and she made no attempt to mimic the stylized gestures of some female singers, who sometimes wore elbow-length gloves to accentuate fluidity. Waldoff wore no gloves, and at times she even stood with her feet planted on the stage in a fixed immobility, with her hands defiantly at her waist, but between verses she sometimes imitated a duck's waddling for emphasis. Her voice was strong, but sometimes harsh.[1]

Waldoff's assumption of a "character" for the purposes of her debut performance was a novel approach. In subsequent performances she appeared as an English schoolboy on holiday, sometimes as a street urchin, sometimes as the flippant, know-it-all Berliner. But behind the personae was the "girl from Gelsenkirchen," the savvy maid from the sooty Rhine-Ruhr region who had made her way to the big city and then conquered it (see Figure 7). It was an obvious inversion of the fashionable style Nelson had cultivated, but the sophisticates at the "new" Roland accepted it. Jelavich (1993: 102) cites numerous sources for this kind of appeal, since it was rooted in the "Berlinesque" tradition of self-deprecation. Waldoff stood on stage "in the correct manner of a pure German maiden … with an incredibly harmless expression; only the eyes occasionally rolled to their corners in horror, as she bawls out ribald, sexually observant songs in a Berlin dialect."

Nelson, in his new venue, enjoyed a success that far exceeded what he had obtained at the Roland, largely because of his continuing good connections with Prince Joachim Albert and the Berlin police. In 1908, Nelson received an invitation for a "command performance" of a cabaret program with two of his performers and himself at the piano for Kaiser Wilhelm II. Thereafter Nelson's venue received a special dispensation from police authorities to remain open after 11:00 p.m. On many evenings, in fact, he did not even open the cabaret until 11:30 p.m. The late hour permitted diplomats from the Foreign Ministry to show up after receptions for visiting dignitaries. They often lingered until the wee hours of the morning, drinking champagne, enjoying the unaccompanied female clientele Nelson attracted, while also partaking in the

Figure 7 *Claire Waldoff. ©Süddeutsche Zeitung/Alamy Stock Photo.*

entertainment on offer. By 1910, Nelson's numerous music publications were earning him considerable income via sheet music sales. One of his best was "Das Ladenmädel" (The Shopgirl), about a ladies' garment clerk in a large Berlin department store. Her male customer makes his way past laces, ribbons, blouses, petticoats with pleats, and finally to lingerie and panties ... He bought a handkerchief, but passed her a note, "Please meet me tonight at 10:00" and named the place. He waited and waited, until at last he heard the rustling of her petticoats ... and she finally appeared. They adjourned to the restaurant and drank their fill of champagne. He was deliriously happy and so was she.

The final stanza made the strong suggestion that she soon was wearing nothing at all. The Kaiser's son, Crown Prince Wilhelm, was so enchanted with the song that he invited Nelson to his residence in Potsdam to perform for his friends. It was one of the many signs that cabaret was climbing up the status ladder. Another popular Nelson song was "Jacques Manasse," about a young woman who worked in a textile firm. She has several encounters with male employees, and upon discovering her pregnancy they form a corporation to provide her with child-support payments, since neither she nor any of her male co-workers knew who the father of her child actually was.

The rumors of war meant an increase in business for some cabarets, but by the summer of 1914 there were lengthy questions in many newspapers about the appropriateness of allowing escapist entertainment to continue. The general consensus among the populace was thought to be confident of a victorious outcome, though in historical retrospect it seems catastrophically nationalistic. Some cabaret venues—Nelson's included—staged militaristic programs in an effort to stir up patriotism. For one such program, Waldoff sang "Immer feste drauf!" (rough translation: "We're with You!") with music by Kollo. Nelson changed the name of his *Chat Noir* to *Zum scharzwen Kater* (Black Cat) and his conférencier Willy Prager opened shows with "We speak German and we want to be German!" The same thing was taking place in Montmartre from the French viewpoint, and Aristide Bruant got into the act, especially after his son was killed in action.

The Outbreak of War

The idea of cabaret performers engaged in patriotic or other kinds of political activity is a much disputed topic. Many historians have argued that a politically conscious cabaret is the best kind of cabaret. Such a cabaret supposedly rises above the entertainment demands of its audience. But a hoped-for marriage of commitment and cabaret entertainment is difficult to consummate. Where gags, punchlines, and economic interests dominate, ideas that go against the prevailing grain are usually absent. Sometimes they do emerge, always hopeful of some small sign of acceptance. Such was the case about 1912, when Kurt Hiller's Das neue Club (The New Club) opened in the Nollendorf Casino in Berlin's Nollendorf Platz. Kurt Hiller (1885–1972) was a committed pacifist and active in Germany's first homosexual-rights organization; his goal was to organize a venue dedicated to the presentation of advocacy reports, poetry, and sketches for the edification of his audience.

In 1911 Hiller had helped to open Cabaret GNU, which featured music by Arnold Schönberg and other composers using the twelve-tone scale; the poetry recited there was said to infer the coming apocalypse, creating a "universal exhilaration in the form of panic laughter" (Senelick 1989: 186). Cabaret, Hiller stated, was the appropriate medium for such performances because of its "vitality" and its ability to create a "sense of experience." It was to be an "adventure of the intellect." Unfortunately, the audience for such adventures was far too small and the organizers soon fell to squabbling. Police halted GNU's activities in 1914 on grounds of blasphemy.

Blasphemy was one of several infractions the authorities used to curtail cabaret activities with the outbreak of the First World War in August 1914. When German troops crossed the Belgian border on August 4, authorities actually closed theaters, concert halls, cabarets, and cinemas in Germany and Austria-Hungary. When it became clear that the troops would not return by Christmas 1914, most venues re-opened and assumed a stance of nationalistic fervor. Nelson lost his lease on the *Chat Noir*, but he managed to lease two other cabarets in 1914 and 1915, the Metropol Cabaret and the Cabaret Sanssouci. He ran them both simultaneously, presenting several numbers praising the Kaiser and troops of the Central Powers allied with him. "Der Kaiser rief" (The Kaiser Called) was one popular tune, but two others were particularly vicious. One was "Hassgesang gegen England" ("Hymn of Hatred against England") by Ernst Lissauer (1882–1937) and "Gehet, Stiefel, tretet Feinde nieder" ("March Boots, Crush the Enemy Beneath You") by Marcel Salzer. Police noted that performances of the "Hymn of Hatred" were more popular than "March Boots."

A common impulse among belligerent nations in the First World War was the politicization of performance. Neutrality or indifference toward the war effort became virtually impossible during those years and press censorship became an operating principle.

But the wartime factor that diminished attendance at cabaret (and other outposts of popular entertainment) was not enthusiasm for the war effort nor was it the censorship that indiscriminately banned all negative reports about the war. It was instead a lack of food, which ultimately turned into wholesale starvation. The British Royal Navy had effectively blockaded German ports on the North Sea, and domestic farm production could not feed both soldiers and civilians.

By the end of October 1918 there were mutinies aboard German naval ships in Bremen and Kiel, followed by popular uprisings in Munich, Hamburg, Bremen, and other cities.

The New Republic

Given the chaos that followed defeat in the First World War, it is sometimes difficult to grasp how cabaret came to enjoy what many believe were its finest years of accomplishment. Never before nor since has there been a livelier cabaret scene in Germany than during the years 1918–33. The collapse of the imperial monarchy ushered in a lengthy period of chaos, violence, anxiety, and suffering. But it also brought the abolition of censorship, to which artists responded in an avalanche of new performance material and styles. The republican constitution that went into effect in August 1919 declared that "censorship will not take place in the new republic." But Article 48 of the constitution contained an "Emergency Decree" provision, which empowered the president's office to ban anything bureaucrats found objectionable. In 1924, they issued a decree that performances which "aroused improper curiosity, that appealed to inappropriate tendencies," or that "accommodated arousal of the senses" could be subject to the jurisdiction of the proper authorities. In the years before that decree, however, formerly insurmountable barriers of artistic expression fell by the wayside, revealing previously illegal extremes of political criticism, polemical humor, punch lines rooted in contemporary experience, gags, nudity, and sexual frankness.

Cabaret, however, rarely became the civic forum that many intellectuals had envisioned for it and toward which activists aimed their efforts. It remained a site of amusement artistry, which at times spoofed various legislators, legal technicalities, party platforms, and bureaucrats. And it certainly extended its reach far beyond the entertainment districts which it had earlier occupied. Its extended reach was made possible by the development of radio broadcasting, the increasing sale of musical recordings, and the expanding market of electric phonograph machines throughout German-speaking Europe. In other words, the so-called Golden Twenties had little gold to offer. Likewise meager were cabaret's contributions to political engagement, to the promotion of social justice, or even offering a concrete challenge to a system that emerged in the wake of the Kaiser's 1918 abdication and his flight into permanent exile. Most political satire subsequently fell into the hands of political activists who prized propaganda and consciousness-raising over art. A lot of what passed for small-venue entertainment transferred to larger venues that were no longer cabarets but variety shows.

Berlin's nightlife initially suffered from the failed Spartacist uprising in January 1919, which was a broad-scale Communist-led insurgency that aimed to take control of all newspaper publishing in Berlin, along with the city's telegraph facilities. As cabaret revived, its artists took different positions in relation to the new republic and the rightwing forces that opposed it. Kurt Tucholsky (1890–1935) had served in the German armed forces. He had been admitted to the German bar as a lawyer, but the war had instilled in him a deep sense of powerlessness and resignation. His outlet was satirical writing. Soon after the war he became the editor of the humor magazine *Ulk* ("Jokester") and by 1920 he was editing a journal with a much wider circulation, *Die Weltbühne*. In articles for that journal he endorsed the new republic, insisting that the danger of rightwing extremism was both real and present.

Walter Mehring (1896–1981) was another apologist for the republic, and his work became the most politically dedicated among writers for cabaret. His wartime service included two years as an artillery corporal, and the experience concomitantly taught him the importance of debunking inherited power and rulership. Like Tucholsky, he found that humor was among the more effective weapons against enemies of the republic. Among the cabaret performers who voiced anti-republican sentiments (and won the admiration of right-wing extremists such as Hitler) was Weiss Ferdl (Ferdinand Weisheitinger, 1883–1949), whose reactionary fables and antisemitic prejudices helped to solidify anti-republican sentiment in the minds of many audiences. He was not alone in his work as a right-wing humorist who attacked the republic and voiced longings for the "good old days" of censorship, official persecution of homosexuals, and the comfort of other "Teutonic values." Ferdl's was nevertheless one of the funnier voices that ridiculed the republic and the newly installed democratic system. A good example is the following: "Equality is a nifty slogan: All that belongs to you belongs to me as well. But what belongs to me I keep hidden, so you can go to hell!" And another: "The housing shortage is a phony show, and with it all the shame of it. Capitalism is the name of it: And everybody gets his own château! Universities are now replete with workers' kids—how sweet! Somebody made a firm decree that everybody gets a Ph.D.!" This kind of palaver proved humorously acceptable to millions via radio, and by the mid-1920s Ferdl often became an opening act for Nazi rallies.

Paul Graetz (1889–1937) had been an actor at Max Reinhardt's Deutsches Theater for four years when in 1920 he started working as an emcee at Reinhardt's second manifestation of the Noise and Smoke cabaret in Berlin. Graetz's ability to extemporize on the texts he had written for himself was matched by the improvisational piano stylings of Friedrich Hollaender, who often accompanied Graetz's singing. All Graetz needed to launch himself and his audience on an imaginary tour of the new republican Berlin was an imaginary cap situated sideways on his head. In some of his routines, he became a taxi driver. "Welcome to the capital of the new republic," he'd begin. "Wait—did I say 'republic'? Excuse me for using such a hard word. If you're out on the street and you hear repeated noises that sounds like 'republic,' just stay calm. It's probably just somebody shooting off a machine gun somewhere. Using human beings for target practice—but they're only factory workers. Plenty more where they came from." This kind of humor proved too pointed for many audiences. The new Noise and Smoke lasted for only a year, and Graetz tamed down his routines to become one of the more well-known performers in several Berlin Cabaret venues, the Kabarett der Komiker (Kadeko) most notable among them.

The Naked Body of Cabaret

In the Wilhelmine years, German police censors had banned nudity, although both *Variété* and *Tingel-Tangel* genres had started to offer "clothed imitations" of the Folies Bergère (see

Heinrich-Jost 1982). In 1907, the Folies-Bergère featured a pantomime called *La chair* (Flesh), which displayed young women in costumes that revealed their bare breasts. From then on, most Parisian revues copied the practice. In 1919, completely nude women appeared in a revue called *Paris que danse* (Paris Dancing) at the Casino de Paris. In Berlin, however, nude dancing was subject to severe penalties. There had certainly been strip-tease entertainments in Berlin and other cities before the First World War, but with the collapse of civic order in late 1918 displays of nudity in a wide variety of venues became commonplace. Proprietors used names for their venues like "Strip Club," "Honky Tonk," "Low Dive," "The Bearded Clam," or "The Bang-Bang Bar." Most women who performed in such places did so without artistic impulse, nor did they possess dance training. What motivated them was a desire simply to make a little money and perhaps survive. One of the most well-known was Cäcilie Funk (1889–1969), who became known as Celly de Rheydt at the suggestion of her husband, Alfred Swedeloh. He had served in the trenches during the First World War but could find no gainful employment after demobilization. He and his wife founded the Ballet Celly de Rheidt and began organizing *Schöneitsabende* ("beauty evenings"), during which Celly and other young women danced to recorded music by opera composer Richard Wagner (1813–83). They were clad mostly in diaphanous scarves. Some critics denounced the show, calling it a "shameless presentation" that debased the monumental stature of Wagner. It was an indication of how a combination of postwar despair and degradation had engendered the previously unthinkable idea of incorporating nakedness and Richard Wagner into the same show (Haustedt 2013: 15). Swedeloh believed that commingling female nudity with Wagner's music made perfect sense. The dances "served to rejuvenate the shattered German nation," he said (in Hughes 2009: 325). It was obvious, however, that he was merely trying to affix a patina of respectability on what was prurient, and it beneficially produced needed income for himself and others in the process. Police reports indicated that Swedeloh charged exorbitant prices for all beverages served at performances. In Munich, police arrested the whole company on charges not of nudity but of blasphemy. They had presented a program titled "Die Nonne" (The Nun), in which the performers appeared in nuns' habits, then removed them to reveal themselves completely naked except for their rosary beads. In the ensuing dance (according to police reports), Celly used a crucifix as an obscene prop, which made the whole program doubly blasphemous.

Anita Berber (1899–1928) was, according to one of her many devotees, a nude dancer who projected "the single most decadent personality in a world that repudiated all moral boundaries or legal restrictions" (Gordon and Droste 2006: ii). The general consensus was that her premature death at age twenty-eight (of both tuberculosis and drug addiction) was a result of having lived a life "riddled by horror, vice, and ecstasy." Another admirer, on the other hand, has observed that Berber owed her fame as a nude dancer in large part to her life offstage; she "performed dances inspired by her addictions. Far from being artificial productions, which asked for the audience's suspension of disbelief, Berber's performances were a way of experiencing the excitement and titillation of being in her world" (Hughes 2009: 327). In baring her personality in her performances, this interpretation maintains that she offered a more intimate experience to those who viewed not just an exposed body, but an exposed persona. That conclusion is highly intellectualized, but it provides a kind of cultural signal about the Weimar Republic's temporary dispensation of censorship, along with its embrace of despair and degradation.

By 1922 the anger and revulsion in the wake of the German defeat in the First World War had not diminished—in fact, it had increased. According to master of ceremonies Fritz Grünbaum (1880–1941), all you had to do

to become a successful master of ceremonies was to stand up in front of an audience of people (who were otherwise happy enough simply to drink and talk with each other) and start bellowing about the betrayal Germany had suffered, how one of these days "we'll settle scores with them [the Americans, British and French. Squint your eyes and imagine you see a profiteer-type in a starched shirt and tuxedo, and you tell him. We were undefeated! We were raped! The men in uniform got stabbed in the back!"

And the main thing, Grünbaum concluded, "is that every sentence must contain the word 'German' at least three times" (in Veigl 2019: 17). Even the doting father of German cabaret, Baron Ernst von Wolzogen, got into the act. In his 1921 book of lyrics, he intoned, "German teeth, learn to bite! / Learn to hate, O German heart!"

Tucholsky termed such poetasting "hell-raising humor," then mocked it with his own form of hell-raising:

The good old days, right? When a loaf of bread cost only two cents, and everybody was nice and polite. There was plenty of coal to heat the house. Both ham and beer were cheap—and nobody paid taxes! But today? There's no Kaiser ... but bread is expensive. And butter? Nobody can afford it. And who can pay the rent? I tell you: the old days are gone forever!

To thunderous applause, he then announced, "the sound of your applause is a hundred thousand smacks up the side of the head you are giving to yourselves!" Tucholsky, Mehring, Klabund, Kästner, and other gifted writers discovered they were preaching to the converted when they made such assertions. The right-wing wave of revanchism, along with unprecedented financial crises, swept over them and drowned their hopes, one by one. Tucholsky and the others wanted "another" Germany, a republic worthy of the name. "Our country is divided," Tucholsky observed and noted that he and his friends were a small part of it. The early 1920s were not comfortable, with their organized acts of terror and previously unimaginable levels of monetary inflation. Those who could survive this wanted and needed entertainment. "You only live once, and that's today" was a typical sentiment heard in Berlin. The war had severely weakened restraints on sexual excess, and there was little effectiveness in previous legal discouragements of promiscuity. Sexual liberty was glorified, drug use was acceptable, and "living for the moment" became a catchphrase to describe the nightlife of most big cities, especially Berlin. Walter Mehring used an "expressive-abbreviated" patois to describe the situation, often using word fragments taken from street jargon and advertisements to capture the "Berlin atmosphere" in his song lyrics. The effect was a kind of snapshot caught in the glare of bright lights, capturing spontaneous moments both hidden and public. The subject matter ironically resembled that of Aristide Bruant: life in the gutter among the pimps and hookers was noble and worthy of literary treatment. A widely circulated poster, pasted on walls throughout the city, proclaimed, "Berlin, stop! Come to your senses: your dance partner is death!" Such lines, Mehring claimed, came from the scribbling he had read on the walls of toilets in various Berlin cabarets.

Wildness and Megalomania

Cabaret of the early 1920s became famous not only because of its superb writers such as Mehring and Tucholsky, but in equal measure because of two remarkable women, namely Rosa Valetti (1876–1937) and Trude Hesterberg (1892–1967). Valetti was Jewish and died in exile; Hesterberg became a Nazi and prospered. Both gathered around them an assortment of talented writers, performers, and musicians, all of whom wanted a departure from the Rudolf Nelson-style "amusement" cabaret in sophisticated evening wear. Their goal was to create a political and literary cabaret which addressed contemporary concerns. They sought to confirm the idea that a politically committed, artistically oriented cabaret could survive and prosper in the new German republic, and to a moderate, albeit brief extent, they succeeded.

Valetti was already an established character actress in theater and film when she opened the *Café Grössenwahn* (Megalomania) cabaret in December 1920. In the late 1890s she had traveled to Paris for study with Aristide Bruant at his cabaret *Le Mirliton*. There she seems to have developed her distinctive baritone singing voice, which in later years was effective particularly in lyrics by Tucholsky, set to music by Friedrich Hollaender. Her Berlin venue was situated on the Kurfürstendamm, above the former Café des Westens, which had been a popular meeting place for writers, theater directors, designers, painters, and composers in the Wilhelmine years. She gave many young performers their start, including the phenomenal Gustaf Gründgens (1899–1963), who later became one of Berlin's most accomplished performers, both as a song-and-dance man and in plays by Goethe and Shakespeare. Kathe Kühl also made her debut at the Megalomania, and for her Valetti's writers composed lyrics for her interpretation. Blandine Ebinger (1899–1993), however, was perhaps the most remarkable of the vocalists at the Megalomania. She debuted with a remarkable song titled "I'm Bumbling around with the Bees," with lyrics by Klabund and music by Edmund Nick (1891–1974). "My mother lies in bed, she's giving birth to my sister, and my other sister's off to church because we're Catholics. Sometime tears drop from my eyes and my heart beats fast, so I just bumble around with the bees" (Klabund 1927: 12–13). She goes on to sing about a pimp who comes to the house and wants her mother's money; her father sits for the sixth time in nearby Plötzensee prison; and she thinks about her boyfriend Emil, who was recently hanged, just as three roosters crowed at dawn.

The above transliteration fails to capture the full pathos of the song, but one must imagine the impact it had on an audience, viewing and listening to Ebinger, a slight and vulnerable-looking figure who had begun her career as a child performer. Much of her childlike demeanor remained in her performances. One of her best songs was "Oh Mond" (O Moon), whose words and music her husband Friedrich Hollaender had written for her. In the song, she asks the moon for protection on her way home late at night. She can feel the moon keeping an eye on her, "just like my papa does when he's sleeping on the sofa." She pleads with the moon for consolation—he knows the sorrows big and small a young girl must endure. "But moon," she sings to her "papa," "Stop looking at me that way. You're trying to seduce me!"

Though attendance at the Megalomania was usually sold out every night, the money Valetti collected at the box office was mostly worthless the next day. The ruinous inflationary monetary policy the German government had inaugurated in 1920 debased the German Reichsmark in geometric proportions. Valetti had no money to pay for water or electricity, and in December 1922 she abandoned the property.

Trude Hesterberg (1892–1967) began her attempt to compete with Valetti beginning in the summer of 1921 with the Wilde Bühne ("Wild Stage"). She had begun her career singing soubrette roles in operetta, which she continued to do as she began to get roles in silent films. Her work with Hollaender, Tucholsky, and Mehring began while singing at Reinhardt's second Noise and Smoke in 1919. She "belted out her chansons as if from a well-oiled Browning," according to critic Kurt Pinthus (in Trautwein 2008). She hired Werner Richard Heymann as her house composer at the Wild Stage, providing music for the lyrics her writers provided. One of her writers was a budding young poet named Bertolt Brecht (1898–1956), but he required no musical help, as it turned out. Like his idol Frank Wedekind, he composed his own music and accompanied himself on the lute.

Berlin was not a city to wallow in self-pity. The more difficult the times in which Berliners lived, the more they demanded revelry, fun, diversion, and hoopla. That was true during the worst periods of the Great Inflation, when a pound of butter cost RM 3 billion. Berliners loaded up bank notes in wheelbarrows to go grocery shopping. It was during this period that the "great cabaret die-off" started. Ensembles with contracted performers who specialized in political satire died first, followed by venues that presented stale jokesters and nude dancing. Dance bars, pick-up joints, and amusement hangouts replaced most of them, because the proprietors of such establishments arranged rent payments on a nightly basis.

The Follies of Foliés and Revues

What replaced most cabarets when they closed were venues that presented "cabaret-style entertainments." They were actually musical extravaganzas that imitated the Folies Bergère in Paris, the Ziegfeld Follies in New York,[2] and the Shubert topical revues called "Passing Shows," also in New York. Like their counterparts in Paris and New York, the Berlin spectacles took place in facilities that could accommodate at least 1,000 patrons: the Comic Opera in the Behren Strasse, the Renaissance Theater in Knesebeck Strasse, the Scala in Luther Strasse, and the Admiral's Palace Theatre in Friedrich Strasse. Also like their French and American equivalents, these shows had six primary ingredients: (1) elaborate settings, (2) star performers, (3) dancing girls, (4) scantily clad girls, (5) wardrobe girls, and (6) cigarette girls. Some observers have described such places in English as "fleshpots" or in German as *Fleischrevuen* ("flesh revues"). The competition among the providers of such fare was intense. James Klein was among the first to stage them at the Comic Opera, with *Berlin ohne Hemd* (Berlin Goes Topless), *Sünden der Welt* (Sins of the World), *Zieh' dich aus!* (Get Your Clothes Off!), and *Donnerwetter—1,000 Frauen!* (Hot Damn—1,000 Women!) (Traub 2010: 138). Producer Herman Haller countered Klein with shows at the Admiral's Palace Theatre, presenting *Drunter und Drüber* (literally "Under and Over," but often loosely translated as "Haywire"), *Noch und Noch* ("Keep on Keeping On"), and *Schön und Schick* ("Gorgeous and Chic"). At Reinhardt's Grosses Schauspielhaus, Erik Charell staged similar extravaganzas (though his audiences at times exceeded 3,000 patrons per night) with titles like *Vom Mund zu Mund* (From Mouth to Mouth) featuring Wilhelm Bendow[3] and Paul Morgan.[4]

The easy comparisons of the Berlin extravaganzas with their American counterparts fueled several debates at the time about the perceived "Americanization of entertainment" in Germany, especially during the five-year period between 1924 and 1929, when economic activity returned to normal levels, joblessness decreased, and political strife seemed to be on the wane. The closest American analogue to Klein, Haller, and Charell was Jacob Shubert (1879–1963), given his excessive penchant for staging female nudity.[5] Ziegfeld did not feature nudity directly, but his shows were instrumental in glorifying the "ideal American girl"[6] and in "loosening the corset"; Haller's antidote to the thin-waisted ideal of the prewar period was the Tiller Girls (Jansen 1987; Kothes 1977).

The Tiller Girls have come in for hefty criticism, because they "sold youth and beauty" and traded on "uniformity of body, costume and pose. These girls of similar stature hold their bodies in linear, angular shapes, linking arms and legs, resulting in images that make it difficult to distinguish one girl's limbs from another" (Hughes 2009: 322). Such chorus lines began in the 1890s in London with the "Gaiety Girls." The Tiller Girls likewise developed in the 1890s, but in Manchester. An eye-witness to the Tiller Girls wrote that their popularity had little to do with the fall of old inhibitions and taboos, however. They were merely imports, a product of businessmen who "worked on the principle that meat shops always make money." Of their contribution to shows at the Admiral's Palace Theatre, he concluded,

> The sensual journey on board the Admiral never leads to a land of bad taste, [but] into a realm where everything is miraculous and fascinating. Surprising scenic tricks, fantastically beautiful costumes, extreme precision of choreography (with the machinelike exactness of the Tiller Girls serving as a regulating metronome): the whole is a

feast for the eye. Beauty becomes a refined manifestation of decadent culture. It is ... a lavish extravagance and always beyond merely sexual. Nudity, presented by the most rigorously selected, most perfect female bodies, is only sparsely employed and always used to heighten the beauty of a particular scene.

(Kuckhoff 1928: 5)

Another eye-witness, the contemporary critic Siegfried Kracauer (1899–1966), voiced sentiments that reflected his search for a symbol that represented the end phase of bourgeois capitalism. He thus interpreted chorus lines as vehicles that conveyed "precisely and openly the disorder of society .... In the streets of Berlin one is, if not infrequently, struck by the realization that all of a sudden everything might split apart one day. The amusements to which the public throngs should also have that effect." Kracauer believed that "the Berlin public behaves in a profoundly truthful manner when it increasingly shuns conventional forms of high arts ... and shows its preference for the superficial luster of revues and production numbers. Here, in pure externality, it finds itself; the dismembered succession of splendid sensory perceptions brings to light its own reality" (Bloch 1962: 368–9; Kracauer 1977: 314–15).

These shows were, in effect, an amalgam of operetta, farce, pantomime, cabaret, and vaudeville. "What kind of genre is this?" asked Friedrich Hollaender (see Figure 8). It must be some kind of hybrid, he concluded, and then he decided to join the crowd. He called his hybrid a "revuette," which featured his songs, lyrics, musical arrangements, and his stagings without elaborate scenery or semi-nude young women. His performers included his wife Blandine Ebinger and other performers who, like Hollaender himself, were idealists, firmly convinced (to paraphrase critic Herbert Ihering) that cabaret should present analyses of contemporary concerns in both songs and lyrics (*aktuelle, gesprochene, gesungene Zeit*).

Figure 8 *Friedrich Hollaender in 1930. ©Süddeutsche Zeitung/ Alamy Stock Photo.*

Rudolf Nelson was likewise involved in the revue business. After 1920, he produced a series of revues he had written, with titles like *Total Manoli* (Totally Manoli), *Bitte, zahlen* (Please Let Me Pay My Bill), *Wir steh'n verkehrt* (We Stand Apart), *Madame Revue* (Madame's Revue), and *Es geht schon besser* (It's Getting Better). Unlike Hollaender, however, Nelson cared little for contemporary political or social concerns; instead, he continued his interest in American popular music and culture. Nelson booked bands featuring African American musicians, Josephine Baker and her "Banana Dance," and on occasion allowed Celly de Rheidt and Anita Berber to strut their barely clothed stuff. Nelson avoided political material by dishing up somewhat "spicy" main courses at times, but he followed them with non-objectionable desserts. Nelson's sparkling elegance and Hollaender's mocking frivolity spawned a third masterful innovator in the revue business, namely the lyricist Marcellus Schiffer (1882–1932). His parody of the newspaper business, titled *Die fleissige Leserin* (The Diligent Reader), with music by Paul Strasser, at the Renaissance Theater, was so popular that it ran for two years. Marcellus Schiffer alternated it with Hollaender's *Hetärengespräche* (Conversations among Courtesans). Composer Mischa Spoliansky (1899–1985) joined Schiffer to create *Es liegt in der Luft* (It's in the Air) at the Komödie Theater on Kurfürstendamm. This production featured Schiffer's wife at the time, French diseuse Margo Lion, and Marlene Dietrich (Maria Magdalena von Losch, 1901–92), who was later to become an international film star singing Hollaender's songs.

Retorts and Tribunals

As noted above, small-venue cabarets had mostly expired by 1922 in Berlin, though in Leipzig the *Retorte* (Rejoinder) hung on until 1923. The *Retorte* did revivals of programs which others had done in Berlin, usually featuring their own versions of material by Mehring, Max Herrmann-Neisse, Joachim Ringelnatz, and Erich Mühsam. A singular talent arose at the *Retorte* in the person of Erich Weinert (1890–1953). A trained illustrator and copy artist, he began writing poems and song lyrics in Leipzig, developing a routine he called the "Distorted Mirror of Events." He moved on to Berlin where, after economic stability returned, several important cabarets were born. First among them were Künstler-Kaffee (Artists' Café, known as "KüKa") and the Kabarett der Komiker (Cabaret of the Comedians, known as "Kadeko"). Weinert joined artists at the Küka, whose number included Werner Finck, later to become the master of ceremonies *par excellence* in Berlin at the *Kabarett Katakombe* (Catacombs Cabaret). The Küka was never licensed as a cabaret, so Weinert felt himself obliged to spoof a wide variety of targets offered him in the new republic, most of them hiding behind "arch-reactionary guises." He often demanded a "reckoning" with the republic's hierarchies, especially those in the military, the universities, and publishers of newspapers. Students, progressive feminists, and other social justice advocates flocked to him at the Küka. Many of his audiences felt that cabaret had finally become what they had desired so fervently: a political tribunal. The Küka's owners did not see things that way. They ordered Weinert off the property, despite (or because of) his ability to attract a crowd. Within weeks, the venue closed for lack of business. Weinert eventually became a member of the German Communist Party (KPD), writing for several agitprop groups. "I felt the need to expose frock-coated patriots right down to their underwear if necessary, who began to assemble under reactionary banners and emblems even before the blood of workers was dry. I wanted to subject them to the ridicule before the entire world" (Weinert 1927). Unfortunately, the world wasn't watching, nor was it really interested.

A central preoccupation of satirists in the mid-1920s like Weinert, Hollaender, and others was exposing the fact that the new German republic was built upon the faulty foundations of the defunct German Empire. The yawning gulf between aspiration and reality was as obvious as the predetermined course toward destruction on which the Weimar republic had already begun to steer itself. It was a course on which nobody wanted to embark, least of all the cabaret artists. "What can satire accomplish, anyway?" asked Kurt Tucholsky, rhetorically (1983a: 666). "Under the Kaiser, we were compelled to think about a republic. And then suddenly, there it was." It was an oddly humorous observation, but nobody was laughing. Tucholsky, Mehring, Kästner, Klabund, and many others nevertheless continued to think about a cabaret suited to a republic. They were idealists, which Tucholsky described as individuals who "want to live in a good world, but live in a bad world. So they beat their heads against badness."

The founders of the aforementioned Kadeko, who were the Viennese comedians Kurt Robitschek (1890–1950) and the aforementioned Paul Morgan, decided against beating their heads and proceeded to create instead a "Cabaret as

Department Store," with a wide variety of wares on offer. Their products included parodies of operetta numbers, satires on contemporary politics, lampoons of hit songs, literary travesties, and serious encounters among or between differing points of view. The venue attracted large numbers of patrons, and "Kadeko" became shorthand for fun that was more than amusing and entertainment that was more than diversion. It was a place where one could pass time in an upbeat atmosphere, often in the company of discerning yet festive audiences. Max Hansen (1897–1961) and Max Adalbert (1874–1933) soon joined the ensemble, as did the aforementioned Werner Finck (1902–78) (see Figure 9). Together they became embodiments of the venue's name, comedians whose humor was somewhat understated and subtle. Their longevity validated their approach, because they and their successors lasted longer (two decades) than any other cabaret on record—even into the years of the Nazi dictatorship.

One of the reasons for their longevity was the strategy to combine elements of cabaret's small-venue intimacy, the sedulousness of a dynamic master of ceremonies, and the show-business appeal of the revue (Budzinski and Hippen 1996: 167). They also did their best to offend almost everybody. The Kadeko's programs, as Jelavich has expertly documented, became targets of protest in 1926, when Berlin newspapers began to publish accusations by Jewish organizations against Jewish comedians telling Jewish jokes at the venue. Among the organizations were Jewish youth groups, Jewish women's organizations, and the Association of Jewish War Veterans, all of whom objected to Robitschek's employment of Jewish dialect humor and parodies of Jewish religious practices. Robitschek and Morgan were themselves Jews, but as one sympathetic observer noted, their exaggerated caricature of certain forms of Jewish speech and practiced by Jews themselves might provide antisemitic ammunition to politicians eager to take advantage of anti-Jewish prejudices among the general public. Many of the organizations issued denunciations of the Kadeko and urged Jews to avoid attending the venue, if

Figure 9 *Werner Finck, ca. 1955. ©Roba Archiv/Alamy Stock Photo.*

possible. "No honorable Jew should support such forms of entertainment," they concluded (Jelavich 1993: 202).

Morgan soon thereafter left the Kadeko troupe to concentrate on film work, and Robitschek moved the group into its stylish new venue in the Mendelssohn Center on Kurfürstendamm.

There he replaced orchestra seating with tables and chairs, but the acoustics were so bad (it had been designed as a cinema) that few could understand what the performers were saying, or singing. His next show, however, with Marcellus Schiffer and music by Mischa Spoliansky, fared much better. It was billed as a "cabaret-opera" titled *Rufen Sie Herrn Plim* ("Call Mr. Plim!"). It was set in a department store, featuring a "whipping boy of all work" Herr Plim, who is constantly getting blamed for everything that goes wrong in the store. It was a parody of operettas, and Spoliansky's best number of the evening was "Heute Nacht oder Nie" (Tonight or Never), with music that perfectly captured the genre's sentimental superficiality.

The Kadeko in many ways summarized all that was best in Berlin's cabaret scene during the late 1920s. Robitschek featured Hesterbeg, Waldoff, Joachim Ringelnatz, Karl Valentin and Liesl Karlstadt, and Margo Lion as regulars, with guest appearances by the venerable Yvette Guilbert. Many believed that Kadeko had actually surmounted politics in its shows, since audiences were made up of socialists, Nazis, communists, nationalists, liberals, moderates, and even Catholics—all sitting under one roof and behaving themselves. The success of Kadeko, however, did not signal to other cabarets that they should follow in its footsteps. The art of an intimate, intellectual, and versatile art form that offered topical commentary started to recede, even as the republic's economy began to improve. Most of the places calling themselves "cabarets" were contrived attempts to alternate the glitter and glamor of revues with stale recapitulations of routines that had been popular elsewhere. Some critics offered funereal salutes to such exercises, noting on the one hand how dated the routines were, and on the other a kind of regret that such routines were no longer current. Others voiced regret that "real" cabaret no longer existed as it once had done or as it should have done. Cabaret had always lived on its contemporaneousness; to regret its lack of same was essentially to say it was dead or dying.

In the wake of the Wall Street collapse of 1929, the Kadeko remained in business. So did the revues of Haller and Charell, though in relatively reduced capacities. There were some tiny "cellar cabarets" located in Berlin and other cities, but they came into and went out of business with a fleeting rapidity that resembled the Aurora Borealis. The most enduring of cabaret-style exercises were those efforts of the German Communist Party to deploy cabaret techniques for the purposes of propaganda. They featured unadulterated, non-diluted programs consisting mostly of Party agitation slogans, jargon, anti-capitalist sketches, anti-Nazi parodies, anti-Socialist diatribes, disputative ballads, and proletarian stereotypes. Most of the Communist performers were amateurs, though many of them were gifted acrobats, tumblers, jugglers, and singers. Few of them were humorists, and the sketches in which they performed were often nothing more than little melodramas. Some Communist agitprop programs were, however, technologically innovative, based on the earlier work of Erwin Piscator (1893–1966). That was true particularly of *Kolonne Links* (The Left Column) and *Rote Raketen* (Red Rockets) in Berlin, *Rote Fanfaren* (Red Fanfares) in Stuttgart, *Rote Rebellen* (Red Rebels) in Chemnitz, and *Rote Ratten* (Red Rats) in Dresden. They used film clips, projections, speeches, lectures, newspaper clippings, exhortations, maps, pamphlet distributions, and re-enactments of historical scenes about revolutions (Hake 2017: 241). Their strategy was to set up the shows quickly, then move on when police or Nazi gangs showed up to disrupt them. The Left Column and other groups received funding from the new Soviet state, but the result was often a diminution of innovative staging and a reliance on "predictable exercises in political indoctrination" (Hake 2017: 242). Alongside these one should take note of non-Communist, leftist-leaning cabarets, such as *Die Wespen* (The Wasps), founded in 1926. They never occupied a fixed venue and toured throughout the republic until 1932, when police authorities banned their performances. Such forced closings were not uncommon in many cities, thanks to the aforementioned Article 48 that allowed "emergency decrees" to halt performances. Erich Weinert was a notable target of

Article 48: police authorities served him with one after another of performance bans, and when cabaret colleagues throughout Berlin began presenting sketches and routines in his defense, the police shut them down, too. When recordings of Weinert's routines began to circulate, the city attorney demanded that Weinert be jailed for four months. He was released from custody when he agreed to withdraw all recordings of his routines from stores that sold them. Then the police hit Weinert with a six-month ban on performing in public, this time throughout the country.

With the financial crisis in the wake of the Wall Street crash deepening, storm clouds ominously gathered on the entertainment horizon. A new soberness pervaded the air, fueled by political, economic, and social instability. Unemployment figures again soared, this time exceeding those of the postwar period. Acute hunger, deprivation, hardship, disease, and adversity made return engagements nearly impossible. Children stopped attending school, trains stopped running on time (when they ran at all), and heavily armed militias from the resurgent Nazi Party and the emboldened Communist Party faced off against each other in broad daylight.

Rosa Valetti tried to keep her small cabaret *Larifari* (founded in 1928) going, though she and co-founder Erich Einegg could not afford a permanent venue. Theirs was an itinerant troupe, featuring mostly Communist songs and sketches intended to arouse proletarian sympathies. The group had its most successful engagements at the Blue Bird, a venue located in Golz Strasse and run by Russian emigres. The most successful venue during the bleak years was The Catacombs, which managed to keep its lease on a venue in Bellevue Strasse. The prime mover there was the aforementioned Werner Finck, whose approach appealed to a "bourgeois-liberal" audience: purposefully naïve yet successfully impudent. Finck's speciality was the sketch that possessed several different levels of meaning at once, but often alternating between gravitas and nonsense. The Catacombs became a parody cabaret, but one that parodied the idea of a cabaret. Many Berliners said they were

sick and tired of the arrogant and snobbish attitudes that many
cabarets possessed, largely because they took themselves way
too seriously. "We, on the other hand, wore cheap department
store suits and scuffed shoes. And those threadbare rags we
used for curtains and backdrops punctured any pretensions we
might have had. Our modesty was unavoidable, our diffidence
was genuine. But we kept our sense of humor. Then something
truly outrageous happened: we became a fad, we were in
vogue." The Catacombs started attracting large crowds, the
only cabaret in Berlin to do so in a regular basis. At very little
expense they achieved substantial effect: parody instead of
propaganda, agreeableness instead of agitation, literary merit
instead of partisanship. Yet as the storm clouds grew darker
and the political winds began to howl, some of Finck's subtlety
went on hold. His routines had a sharper bite:

> Who woke up the baby with hammer pounding? The
> baby's father offers no excuse. And who put a meat cleaver
> in Aunt Frieda's lap? That woman might put the thing to
> use. And who put the wig on Uncle Emil's head? The old
> man looked much better without it. And who taught the
> gold fish how to play the flute? No good person should ever
> be glad about it.

The more boisterous Nazi marches got, the louder and more
audacious became the voices of anti-Nazi cabaret artists like
Finck. But it was too late. There had been warning signs of the
coming Nazi flood, but the voices who spoke loudest against
the Nazis were often the ones who made the least reckoning
with the fates that awaited them. With every outburst, every
plea for reason, every joke about Hitler's moustache, their
chances of survival diminished. One exception was Friedrich
Hollaender, who by 1932 had become cabaret's most
accomplished composer, writer, director, and apologist. He
saw the catastrophe awaiting him and by December 1932 his
suitcases were packed. By the end of February 1933 he was
gone—first to Paris, and three months later to Hollywood.

Hollaender was not a moralist but a survivor. Others who felt the need to form a united front against the Nazis, who deployed weapons of wit, humor, polemics, political analysis, reason, and moralism against the growing tide, found themselves helplessly swept away. Many of them had read the metaphorical writing on the walls of The Catacombs, but in the Kadeko, Robitschek and Kurt Lilien performed a brief sketch on the need for emigration. "Say, I think the time has come for us to really start thinking about emigration." "Emigration?" Lilien asked. "What are you talking about?" "Hitler." "Hitler? What about him?" "Well, you've read *Mein Kampf*, haven't you?" "No!" Lilien protested. "I never read best-sellers."

Both men left Germany soon after this exchange, never to return. Robitschek made it to New York, where he died, using the name of "Ken Robey." Lilien was murdered in the Sobibor extermination camp. Kurt Tucholsky likewise went into exile (where he died in 1935), realizing that the cause for cabaret engaged in harmless routines like the one cited above was hopeless. Cabaret was under a death sentence, he believed, largely due to its middle-class supporters. "The middle class never believe in cruelty," he said. "The reason? They have no imagination."

> "A cabaret without a taste for aggression," Friedrich Hollaender concluded, is a cabaret unfit for survival. This is not a battlefield where the weapons of polished words and saucy music face off against iron and lead. And yet, when you think about it, cabaret is unbeatable. Only in cabaret can you entertain thousands and at the same time administer a poisonous blessed sacrament, hardly noticed by observers, even as the blood starts to percolate through the system and the brain is aroused to the point of actually thinking.

No wonder, then, that the Nazis found Hollaender so retrograde and so contrary to their ideas about culture.

5

The Nazi Terror

Catastrophe

In the years between the financial collapse of late 1929 and the electoral victories of the National Socialist Party in late 1932 (resulting in the appointment of Adolf Hitler to the office of Chancellor in early 1933), a few small-stage revues somehow maintained operations in Berlin. They copied to a large extent the format Rudolf Nelson had developed two decades earlier, though Friedrich Hollaender surpassed Nelson with his "revuette," of which he became the sovereign master, as the author, composer, and director. Film director (and fellow Berliner) Billy Wilder (1906–2002) later said, "For those of us who knew him in Berlin, Hollaender had always been a genius—from head to foot, I swear, a genius" (in Lareau 2000: 113). Hollaender's shows in some respects resembled Irving Berlin's Music Box revues in New York between 1920 and 1924. They included songs, sketches, dances, mimes, and other entertainments with specific dimensions that fit into an overarching idea. A significant departure for Hollaender's was their "clear allusions to current political affairs, in support of pro-republican and anti-militarist viewpoints" (Jelavich 1993: 228).

Like Irving Berlin, Hollaender was drafted into military service in the First World War. He was the son of Viktor

Hollaender, a composer and orchestrator who had worked extensively for German-language theaters and opera companies in Milwaukee and Chicago, but his son Friedrich was born in London, where Viktor was then working at the Opera Comique in the English capital. In 1899 the family moved back to Berlin, where Viktor taught at the Stern Conservatory and worked for Ernst von Wolzogen at his Colorful Theater. By the time he was eighteen, Friedrich was a student at the Stern Conservatory (though not under his father's tutelage), and at age nineteen he received his draft notice. He avoided front-line duty in the trenches, as did Irving Berlin, by composing musical entertainments for soldiers. He served for two years as music director and pianist of the *Theater an der Westfront* (Theater on the Western Front), which performed in French and Belgian venues which the Germans occupied, including Sedan and Lille (in France), along with Ostende and Brussels (in Belgium). The troupe's leader was a non-commissioned officer named Fritz Grunwald, who had been an actor in several musical ensembles before the war and was director of the City Theater in Freiburg. Grunwald had sold the idea of musical entertainment to German commanders in 1916 by insisting that soldiers pay their own way to see shows, rather than expecting officers to provide them free tickets (Pörzgen 1935: 23–8).

In 1919, the German army discharged Hollaender, and Max Reinhardt hired him as house composer for the second version of his Noise and Smoke cabaret, this time located in the cellar of his enormous Grosses Schauspielhaus in Schumann Strasse. There he met and began working on music for several lyricists, among them Klabund, Kurt Tucholsky, and Walter Mehring. He also met (and soon thereafter married) Blandine Ebinger. By 1920 he was working as a freelance composer, completing incidental music for several Reinhardt productions and writing songs for Trude Hesterberg at her Wild Stage and Rosa Valetti at her Megalomania cabaret. During those years the sheet music sales of several Hollaender songs began to soar, as did sales of his recordings. His income from those sources allowed him to continue to compose songs after Hesterberg and Valetti went bankrupt. In 1926 he staged the first of his "revuettes," as he called them, titled "Laterna magika" at the Renaissance Theater. It featured a six-man musical ensemble called the Weintraub Syncopators, but he designated them his "house orchestra." Response to the show was so positive that he staged four others in quick succession. All of them produced hit songs, such as "Raus mit den Männer aus dem Reichstag!" ("Get Men out of the Reichstag!") for Claire Waldoff. In 1929 he agreed to write and conduct the music for a new film starring Marlene Dietrich called *Der blaue Engel* (The Blue Angel), directed by Josef von Sternberg, co-starring Oscar Award winner Emil Jannings (1884–1950).[1] In the movie, the Syncopators are often on screen, with Hollaender at the piano.

Most of the songs Hollaender wrote for the film became popular both in Europe and in America. The best known among them was "Ich bin von Kopf bis Fuss auf Liebe eingestellt," for which Hollaender wrote the music, lyrics, and orchestration. Its English title is "Falling in Love," which Sammy Lerner (1903–89) wrote for the American release.[2] It barely captures the song's somewhat brutal determinism: the transliterated lyrics mean "I'm ready for love from my head down to my toes." Marlene Dietrich became so closely identified with the song that it became, according to some observers, her "anthem" on concert tours, both during and after the Second World War. In it, she confesses that "men swarm around me, like moths to a flame. They see a mysterious glow, a kind of *je ne sais-pas-quoi* look in the eyes of a beautiful woman. But when my eyes look deep into his during our *vis-à-vis*, what are they saying?" They're not saying anything in one interpretation. Like a car made for driving, like whisky made for drinking, she's there for the taking. Hollaender wrote other songs for Dietrich, especially after he left Germany for Hollywood and began working as "Frederick Hollander." For the Paramount and Warner Brothers studios he created over 260 musical works and received four Academy Award nominations. Many critics agree that his most memorable American songs were for the 1939 film *Destry Rides Again* for Universal Studios (for which the future Broadway composer Frank Loesser[3] wrote the lyrics). In it, Dietrich played Frenchy, the somewhat disreputable girlfriend of the saloon owner played by Brian Donlevy. Her numbers in the saloon were "See What the Boys in the Back Room Will Have" and "Little Joe the Wrangler."

Hollaender in 1931 created an ingenious parody of the synchronized chorus line, of which the Tiller Girls were the most familiar and who remained popular in Berlin "cabaret revues." To celebrate the new year, Hollaender opened his *Tingel-Tangel* Cabaret in the cellar of the Theater des Westens on January 7, the same cellar where Trude Hesterberg had located her Wild Stage. It was a small-stage venue visually similar to the one in which Dietrich had held forth as Lola Lola in *The Blue Angel*. His handsome salary for the film work, along with the substantial royalties he continued to earn for the sheet music and recordings of his songs, allowed Hollaender to lease the former Wild Stage venue, and with the Syncopators he began to write material for *Tingel-Tangel*. By 1931, Hollaender was arguably the best cabaret composer in Europe. As noted above, however, he was also a gifted director. For his "chorus girl parody," he employed only two dancers, namely the beautiful von Elben sisters, Grit and Ina. Hollaender fitted between the sisters a kind of "dance machine," composed of nine identical cutout figures, all dressed alike and all connected to each other. The sisters' costumes were likewise identical to the cutouts. The nine cutout figures held between the sisters mimicked their moves, because the cutouts had movable joints that corresponded to the sisters'. When Grit and Ina moved, the cutouts moved in identical fashion with them. It took several days of rehearsal to achieve the effect Hollaender wanted, and on opening night the device functioned perfectly, as all eleven figures moved in identical synchronization. It was an accurate replication of a human kick line, combined with the added force of metaphor: the human figure as mechanical object. It was far more riveting than anything Siegfried Kracauer had written about, namely human mechanical objects and their ability to maintain a "Cult of Distraction" in Berlin (Koss 1996: 80). The effect was a *coup de théâtre* rarely seen in cabaret.

A corresponding effort of significance parallel to Hollaender's was *Die Katakombe* (The Catacombs), whose director was Werner Finck (1902–78). The new establishment opened in the Künstlerhaus, where Max Reinhardt had launched his first Noise and Smoke cabaret in 1901. Alan Lareau has described the place when Finck leased it as a "long, cold cellar paneled in darkened wood, with pillars and a domed ceiling with three or four rows of crude wooden tables." There was a small platform at one end with a wire strung between two columns, from which hung the curtain. The relaxed, somewhat improvised atmosphere was central to the venue's tremendous effect. "Everything was kept informal on stage, among the audience, or behind-the-scenes" (Lareau 1995: 128). It was somewhat amateurish, but intentionally so. It was lowbrow but not vulgar. The curtain rarely functioned properly, and the performers brought on tables, chairs, lamps, or other props as needed (*Berlin am Morgen* 1929). The sets were made of cardboard, and the costumes were nothing more than articles of clothing which performers found in thrift stores. Even the drinks were low priced. The mood was one of relaxation, freedom, and fantasy which had largely disappeared in the late 1920s (Lareau 1995: 132). Finck's intention was to remain cheerful whenever possible in the sketches he wrote, in solo routines for others, and in dance numbers. One of his more well-known humorous monologues onstage came in 1931: "In the first week of the Third Reich all parades through Berlin neighborhoods will come to a halt at the first sign of inclement weather such as rain, hail, or snow. And then, all Jews in the neighborhood will be shot" (McNally 2000: 150). Finck's unique style as a master of ceremonies was based on such futuristic speculations, but also his fictional accounts of events that never happened, with sharp-edged metaphors that proved highly effective. In one such routine he talked about the property he had recently purchased in a fictional town called

"Kuhfort."[4] It was important at his stage in life, he said, to own a piece of property "and the soil beneath it. The soil, but not the blood."[5]

Dance was important in Catacombs programs; "The Hairdresser Dance" is a good example. In it, Hedi Schoop (1906–95) wore five wigs as a means of switching quickly from one to another of five different characters. She became Friedrich Hollaender's second wife in 1932, after he divorced Blandine Ebinger the year previous. She borrowed Hollaender's idea of using life-size cutouts as dancers in one particularly clever routine, titled "Solo Couple Dance." She danced ballroom style with a giant cardboard cutout of a man in formal dress, whose feet were tied to hers. As a couple, Schoop and her "partner" embodied what many considered the impossibility of effective coalition or combined effort in German politics. The idea of political parties working together toward a commonly shared goal had long since disappeared.

Werner Finck often faced accusations of being Jewish, and he usually answered with, "I'm not Jewish. I just look intelligent." His status as a Gentile no doubt assisted him mightily as he continued to run the Catacombs after Hitler and the Nazis assumed power in 1933. Finck quickly realized, however, that the survival of the Catacombs as well as his own depended on an ability to develop strategies of indirect commentary in his routines. He endowed them with different levels of meaning at once, but often alternating between gravitas and nonsense. Among his strategies were: (1) use sentence fragments; (2) employ meaningful words in meaningless sentences; (3) stutter; (4) apply double and triple meanings to political buzzwords to make those words seem silly or even meaningless; and (5) adopt non-committal pronunciation of names and places that were politically taboo (McNally 2000: 151). For example, the Nazis rarely permitted the use of the word "republic" or "democracy" when describing the Weimar structure of government. The word Propaganda Minister Goebbels insisted on was "system." The accepted buzzword for the Weimar years was "the system era." Such usage in English might be "niggardly," which actually means "stingy," but just hearing the word might cause discomfort to some hearers whose primary interest is political correctness. Other analogous usages in English include "bitch," which can be a noun, a verb, or an adjective, but feminists find the word in any context deplorable. Using neologisms that offend can also be humorous. Finck no doubt would have understood the word "zesticular" to describe "toxic masculinity." Other humorous lines that might today arouse dual comprehension: "I'm an equal-opportunity political offender. I don't care whose bullshit you believe," or "It's really sick humor to make jokes about AIDS." As the Nazi dictatorship wore on and linguistic departures had mortal consequences, Finck became a master of making trouble not so much from the meaning of what he said, but from what he didn't say, and in the process he insinuated criticism of the regime.

The National Socialist Reign of Terror

By no means did cabaret disappear under the Nazi dictatorship. Most Nazis liked cabaret, just as they liked theater, movies, and film. Their brutal treatment of cabaret artists, actors, singers, comedians, and other performers is, however, well documented. Ulrich Liebe has amply demonstrated that such individuals were more than victims; they were the prey of a terror barely imaginable at the time and nearly impossible to describe today. Many of them were entertainers who relieved the average person of his cares and woes. How many thousands of people felt better after seeing these people perform? Add to their number (some have estimated that over 4,000 performing artists perished under various Nazi usages and practices) the banal and gross indignity of their anguish and torment. Extraordinary, once-heralded performers were subjected to begging for soap from concentration camp authorities. Actresses in their seventies were hauled off to barracks with hideously unsanitary conditions; families split up; the "insolence of office," as Hamlet called it, heaped insult and injury on indignities that nobody deserved.

Some of the best cabaret artists experienced work proscription. Storm troopers interrupted Hollaender's performances, mounted the stages where he played, and spat on him. Others who had worked in cabaret since the early days of the century (such as Rudolf Nelson) escaped Germany but landed in nearby countries, where they lived dangerously—many of them in hiding. Most of those capable of leaving Germany in 1933 did so almost immediately after Hitler assumed the office of Reich Chancellor.

Those who remained often attempted to continue their careers. Some cabaret artists openly declared their intention to fall into line with the new regime, or at least offer nothing that anyone could construe as politically objectionable. Willi Schaeffers (1884–1962) was one of them, as his work as emcee at Berlin's Kadeko bears witness. He remained at the Kadeko until Goebbels closed down all venues of public entertainment in 1944. Schaeffers proudly placed a large placard in the venue's foyer that announced "Admission to Jews Strictly Forbidden!" Other opportunists saw the new regime as a vehicle for professional advancement. They publicly placed themselves at Goebbels' disposal and noticeably prospered. Among the most observable of such opportunists was Trude Hesterberg, who had joined the Nazi Party before the new regime was elected, and by December of the regime's first year in power she opened her own venue. She christened it the *Musenschaukel* (The Muses' Swing), where she offered up what she claimed was non-political material.

Finck found a temporary *métier* at the Catacombs, despite frequent denunciations from private citizens and random, unpredictable Gestapo investigations. Finck's case is a curious example of how some performers remained on the precipice of incrimination. To some in the Nazi leadership he appeared to be cooperative; to others he was a dangerous maverick. Among his somewhat deceptive routines was his supposed purchase of a small freehold outside Berlin. In his aforementioned routine about the "blood and soil" property he had purchased, he described it

> as a relatively small property. Two views of the east from the west, one of the west from the east. That's already quite a lot to talk about. But the property has little trees. Little apple trees. But they're so young, they still have to go to tree school. Nowadays everything gets sent off to school, even the trees, so they will learn what a tree family is, and what's a family tree. That way, there are no misunderstandings. And then, there is a fence around everything ….

He was referring to the Reichstag's passage of the "Nuremberg Laws" of 1935: the Reich Citizenship Law and the Law for the Protection of German Blood and German Honor.[6] Aryan identity cards were required of all inhabitants living on "German soil." Tracing one's family tree was crucial in the process. Having one Jewish grandparent was enough to identify one as a *Vierteljude* or "quarter Jew." Finck identified himself on his little farm as a questionable presence on German soil, especially as he strolled at night through its little pastures:

> Nightly in the grassy pasture, several large cows go to graze, to chew, and do what cattle do. No objection do they seem to raise If on my way I hustle through. If they wanted, they could trample me. If they thought about it. But to be exact, they really don't think that much. And anyway, they're not easy to distract.

The cattle he encounters in the pasture are obviously the principalities and powers who rule the place, and he does his best not to disturb them: "So, quietly I go among the crowd, walking on the grass they're eating, hurrying, hoping not be too loud, and slightly worried, my heart beating, wondering if my situation is depleting."

His situation was indeed depleting, though he did not yet realize it. By 1935, Finck had appeared as an entertainer at numerous Nazi Party gatherings, but there were murmurings that he was becoming problematic. A good example of what Goebbels called his "deception" was a routine he did with Ilse Trautschold (1906–91), in which she began to make a charcoal line drawing of a famous person whose last name began with "Goe." Finck wandered, looked at the drawing (unseen by the audience), and makes laconic comments. Everyone assumes the drawing is of Herman Goering, and some gasps filled the air as Finck continued to ridicule the figure as an "egotist," a "braggart," and "overrated." Then Trautschold revealed to the audience the image she had drawn, and it turned out to be that of Johann Wolfgang Goethe. The audience exhaled in relieved laughter. Finck also said things about "secret police" operatives among his audiences, such as "They are not really that secret. I can see them here tonight, and it's no secret what they're doing." He nevertheless maintained support among some influential Nazis. The editors of the Party's official newspaper, the *Völkischer Beobachter*, for example, praised the Catacombs' new program in 1935 as "a joyful evening, full of witty and jocular merriment." They described Finck as a kind of court jester, spreading good humor around, often with "surprising" punch lines. Yet his tendency to test the boundaries of humor caused other Nazi ideologues to look for implicit meanings behind his shenanigans. They accused Finck and his colleagues of uttering "typical Jewish-liberalistic witticisms," engaging in "political well-poisoning," and even "engaging in snide remarks indirectly aimed at the government" (in *Der Spiegel* 1966: 168). They were of course correct in such accusations. Less correct was the observation that the Catacombs audience consisted mostly of what appeared to be "non-Aryan" individuals. There were recommendations that Goebbels close down the Catacombs and put Finck and some of his equally troublesome fellow performers in what they euphemistically termed "protective custody." Goebbels followed those recommendations in late May 1935. Gestapo agents arrested Finck and sent him to the Esterwegen concentration camp (about 60 miles west of Bremen) for a term of six weeks.

The brevity of his confinement in Esterwagen was a result of the enmity between Hermann Goering (who at the time was prime minister of Prussia and thus had jurisdiction over Berlin and its entertainment industry) and Goebbels (whom the Hitler cabinet had placed in charge of all matters regarding the performing arts). Goering actually liked the charcoal drawing sketch and ordered Finck released from custody and given a trial. More than a year later (in October 1936), a Berlin court demanded that Finck perform some of the sketches which had been so offensive. He did so, and there was enough convincing laughter among the judges to convince them that no offense had taken place. They officially declared him innocent of all charges.

Such measures against cabaret artists were intended as warning shots to everybody concerned, and eventually only Kadeko remained. Goebbels, however, arranged for a cabaret called Tatzelwurm (an eerily appropriate title, meaning "cryptid worm") to occupy the Catacombs' former venue. Goebbels then arranged for an article about the closings published in *Das schawarze Korps*,[7] running the headline "Two Whorehouses Forced to Close." Goebbels nevertheless continued to attend cabaret performances at the Kadeko and the Cryptid Worm, "laughing until my sides were splitting" (Fröhlich 1998: 223), while concomitantly reading Gestapo reports or complaints from anonymous sources that somebody, somewhere, might have exceeded regime-imposed boundaries for appropriate cabaret humor. Goebbels hoped that establishing a new cabaret in the Catacombs' premises would encourage others to open venues in line with what the regime wanted. One of the results was *Die acht Entfesselten* (The Unchained Eight), which consisted of four couples who toured throughout Nazi Germany dressed in evening wear and singing inoffensive songs.

Among other cabaret performers who found favor with the regime was the aforementioned Weiß Ferdl, who had gotten to know Hitler personally in 1921. Ferdl was by then fairly well-known in the Munich area and accompanied Hitler on speech-making tours in the early 1920s. Hitler also used Ferdl as his "opening act" at some venues, hoping that Ferdl's humor would get the crowd in the mood for the ranting and raving to follow. Later, after Hitler was named chancellor, the two often had afternoon tea in the Reich Chancellery, though Ferdl did not become an official Nazi Party member until 1940. By then, however, even he was beginning to grow somewhat impatient with the Nazi regime. In one routine, he mentioned that "it was clear that the German populace is 98 percent behind Hitler." What surprised him was that on the street, "I am always running into that dubious two per cent" (Large 1998: 375).

Cabaret received little direct subvention from Goebbels' Propaganda Ministry, but the numerous performers promised employment by the Kraft durch Freude (Strength through Joy) organization failed to materialize.[8] The Strength through Joy organization and its sister agency the Deutsche Arbeitsfront[9] (German Labor Front, which replaced all independent trade unions) were in the portfolio of Robert Ley.[10] He claimed that Hitler's genius would eventually bring about Nazi conquest of the moon and all the planets in the solar system. "Cabaret," Ley insisted, "can do nothing more than help one to relax and recuperate. And I can say personally, that after an evening laughing myself silly and enjoying myself, I feel completely restored. I can live on that for the next 14 days. And that's true for many others as well." Goebbels agreed: "[We Germans] want to laugh and we like to laugh, but not about things we hold sacred and with great conviction we have struggled to achieve" (in Jelavich 1993: 241). The warning was clear: cabaret artists should do more than exercise caution. They had to be harmless.

By 1937, Finck was back at work as a performer, this time for Willy Schaeffers at the Kadeko, but in early 1939 Goebbels had Finck's membership in the performing artists' guild revoked. The routine that got Finck in trouble again was about an informal soirée he had recently attended: "There was a party the other night, and somebody told a funny joke. Others joined in. 'But my friends,' I said, 'the window is open, and we're talking pretty loud. Maybe it's best to shut it.' 'If I could be quite open with you,' the window wanted to say at that moment, hoping to join the conversation. But the window could only growl; it couldn't speak. Walls are much better at joining human conversations, because they, at least, have ears." Goebbels denounced any effort that dared even to make unspoken jests (which were Finck's specialty) about Gestapo tactics. Political jokesters were nothing but a "residue of liberalism," he said. To avoid another stretch in a concentration camp, Finck volunteered for military service in 1939 and was trained as a radio operator, just in time for the German invasion of Poland and the onset of the Second World War.

Cabaret in Exile

Cabaret in Austria (before the Nazi takeover of the country in 1938) enjoyed a traditional ruling that venues with fewer than fifty seats were immune to police intervention. Any capacity above that number became subject to theater regulation and censorship. The result was a slight increase in employment possibilities for German refugees in Vienna, and cabaret performers realized that emigration to Austria was perhaps the safest means of survival. But even in German-speaking Austria it was difficult to establish a foothold. Kurt Robitschek, founder of the Kadeko in Berlin, tried to re-establish himself with a cabaret revue he called *Wiener Illustrierte* (Vienna Illustrated), but he discovered that cabaret was not an exportable product. Some believed—while others had fervently hoped—that the Nazi pestilence was temporary. How could they assume anything different?

Hitler's triumphal entry into Vienna on March 12, 1938, finalizing the annexation of Austria into the "Greater German Reich," put a quick and often violent end to such hopes. Gestapo officials rounded up as many Jewish performers as they could find, which included Fritz Grünbaum and Egon Friedell mere hours after the annexation became legal. Grünbaum had, as noted in an earlier chapter of this volume, become a successful emcee in Berlin cabarets but had returned to his native Vienna in 1933 to concentrate on film work as a comic character actor. Agents arrested him and sent him to the Bavarian prisoner camp in Dachau, where SS guards who remembered him from cabaret days tortured and finally killed him. His wife later received his ashes in a small urn, along with a bill for his cremation and for costs of shipping and handling. Agents also attempted to arrest Egon Friedell, who had worked with Mark Henry and Marya Delvard at Vienna's Bat cabaret. As they tramped up the stairs of the building where he lived, Friedell opened a large window in his apartment and warned pedestrians below to "get out of the way." He then leaped from the window to his death on the pavement, some 60 feet below.

Of the cabaret artists who managed to get out of the new "Greater German Reich," most crossed borders with empty pockets. They left more than worldly goods behind, however, and they missed more than house and home even if they were lucky enough to find asylum abroad. "We've lost our mother tongue," complained Hollaender in his "Immigrant's Ballad." Cabaret was often untranslatable in, and untransportable to, another country. It wasn't just the tribulations of getting passport visas, the troubles with censors, the struggle for a minimal existence, or the fear of being deported that made life for the emigre so difficult. It was, for example, in America, the complete absence of a cabaret tradition and the non-existence of an audience who might attend their performances. Refugees faced the impossibility of emigrating away from their language, to which their art was inextricably bound.

Impossibility did not stop them from trying. In the first months of their dispersion, several tried their hands at creating "Exile Ensembles." The first one was in Paris, where a bilingual experiment called *Laterne* was forming; Hollaender gave thought to working with the group but it turned out to be an "anti-fascist" mouthpiece which soon folded (Hermann 1981). And in any case, he soon got an offer from Hollywood and departed Europe altogether. A year later, Rudolf Nelson opened his *La Gaîté* venue in Amsterdam, which remained active until the German invasion and occupation of the Netherlands in 1940. In Moscow, members of the *Kolonne-Links* and *Truppe 1931* agitprop troupes reconstituted themselves and presented programs until 1936. In that year many of them were arrested and later executed as part of Stalin's "Great Purge" of Communist Party memberships. Since nearly all members of agitprop troupes were Party members, they found themselves caught up in a dragnet that eventually resulted in the deaths of 4 million Party members. In the Paris *Laterne* program, the performers expressed the wish that they might "arrive at a new awareness of reality, and to act in such a way that reality can conform to our wishes." They, like so many others, were disappointed in their hopes. In Czechoslovakia, several former agitprop performers gathered in Prague to form the Studio 34, but it was an all-German language group, as were "Echo from the Left," "Red Star," and "New Life." In England there were attempts at establishing German-, Hungarian-, and Czech-language entertainments, but they were aimed mostly at uplifting morale. By 1939, there were about 70,000 political refugees in the UK, and some efforts to stimulate English-speaking attendance were moderately successful, though temporary.

The English experience of exile cabaret was unique for another reason, mainly attributable to the British Broadcasting Corporation's reach into Germany and occupied Europe.

Germans, of course, also had radio broadcasting facilities. Shortly after Hitler assumed the office of Chancellor in 1933, his new government took control of two radio stations, which proceeded to fill the airwaves with all manner of Nazi-inspired rigmarole, such as the proper way to offer the "Hitler greeting" (extending the right arm out at 60 degrees, then energetically shouting "Heil Hitler!"). Within a few years, the Nazis owned and operated 100 additional stations. German authorities could not stop foreign radio waves beaming across borders, "but they could make listening to broadcasts emanating from the United Kingdom a crime," according to a recent BBC documentary production.[11] After the declarations of war in 1939, anyone caught listening to the BBC faced a jail sentence, and repeating information heard in a foreign broadcast could result in the death penalty.

The Austrian journalist Robert Ehrenzweig (1904–84), who had an earned doctorate in chemistry and wrote under the name Frank Lucas, found himself working for the BBC in 1940. The corporation's new German Service suggested that Lucas create some kind of humorous program that offered "counter-propaganda" to German listeners on the short wave band. Though he had little previous radio experience, and even less writing and performing comedic material, he invented the role of "Pvt. Adolf Hirnschall." The content of what amounted to a one-man cabaret routine were letters purportedly from a certain Pvt. Adolf Hirnschall, stationed on the front lines with his Reichswehr regiment, to his wife in "Zwieseldorf," a likewise fictional village somewhere in rural Germany or Austria. The program's conceit was that Pvt. Hirnschall read the letters to his fellow soldiers before he mailed them to Zwieseldorf. In the letters, he is an ordinary foot-soldier with unflinching loyalty to the Führer; yet, the tone of the letters is oddly naïve and appealing. Hirnschall (whose name obliquely suggests "empty-headed") is nevertheless so sincere that he unintentionally reveals contradictions in Nazi strategy and the errant stupidity of Nazi leadership, including that of the Führer himself.

Other fanciful programs on the BBC included cabaret sketches by art historian Bruno Adler (1888–1968) that featured two characters named Kurt und Willi. They periodically meet up after work in a tavern to discuss things, and Kurt (a school teacher) is an "average" German who believes everything the government says, while Willi actually works for the Propaganda Ministry. He humorously discloses to Kurt the "story behind the story," providing details of Hitler's strange diet, Goebbels' appetite for young film starlets, and Goering's enormous capacity for food and drink. It was essentially an exercise in debunking. Kurt and Willi did not directly disparage Hitler and the others, but their discussions punctured the cherished Nazi notion of the Führer's invincibility, while demystifying the rest of the leadership's purported dedication to the "will of the people."

Other German refugee performers on the BBC included Lucie Mannheim (1899–1976), who found film work in London. Her most notable film was *The 39 Steps*, directed by Alfred Hitchcock in 1935. Mannheim's version of "Lilli Marleen" on the BBC attracted attention in Berlin, because the original singer of the song, Lale Andersen, had been arrested on charges of complicity in an espionage case. Andersen was a featured performer at Kadeko and had premiered "Lilli Marleen" there in 1939. The composer of the song was Norbert Schultze (1911–2002), another regular at the Kadeko; he took the lyrics from a poem by Hans Leip (1893–1983), a German veteran of the First World War. Andersen later made a recording of the song, which German armed forces radio-aired in 1941 to German troops in Yugoslavia. It became enormously popular with German enlisted men, but Goebbels ordered broadcasters to stop playing the song. Erwin Rommel, commander of German forces in North Africa, liked the song so much that he asked military broadcasters to resume playing it. Goebbels was forced to rescind his ban, and the broadcasts resumed promptly every night at 9:55 p.m., just before sign-off. It later became a favorite of soldiers from several nationalities, especially American and British troops. It was an indication of cabaret's ability to cross over language barriers at least in one respect: sentimental music, longing for home, sung from the heart.

"A good mood is essential in wartime," Goebbels observed in 1942. "Not only is it indispensable, but you cannot win a war without it" (Goebbels 1977). His Propaganda Ministry was in an active state of exertion throughout the war years, sending entertainers to the front lines, to barracks on the home front, to field hospitals both at home and abroad, and to all of the occupied countries where soldiers, sailors, and airmen were stationed. Some entertainers were sent off to concentration camps as inmates, then released and allowed to resume entertaining the troops. Others were regular performers on German armed forces radio broadcasts. Military commanders gave talented enlisted men the chance of temporarily exchanging their weapons for laugh routines. The most well-known example was Werner Finck, whose service in an infantry division won him the Iron Cross for bravery and later the Medal for Service in the East, which Finck later described as his "Frozen Flesh Medallion" (Finck 1966: 76). The division commander soon rescued him from front-line duty as a radio operator, however, and put him in charge of entertaining troops in Italy. Wolfgang Neuss, Peter Frankenfeld, and Lotar Olias were among others who somehow maintained their sense of humor literally in the face of death and destruction. Sometimes soldier/entertainers formed groups and gave themselves military-sounding names: the Jackboots (*die Knobelbecher*) or the Anti-Tank Grenades (*die Panzer-Spreng-Granate*). The astonishing thing about these troupes was the emphasis on group solidarity instead of political correctness. Their commanders were largely responsible for such a development, recognizing that "Berlin was far away," and anything that got laughs was allowed, as long as it wasn't defeatist.

Klaus and Erika Mann

On the first day of 1933, a new cabaret group called *Pfeffermühle* (Pepper Grinder) made their debut in the Munich venue called *Bonbonniere*, not far from the Hofbräuhaus where Hitler and his earliest companions launched their 1923 attempt to overthrow the Bavarian government. This ensemble had no intention of overthrowing anything, but they insisted that Hitler and the Nazis posed a profound threat to all of Europe. They set themselves up as unswerving opponents to the rising Nazi tide that had swept two elections in 1932. The first one (in July 1932) resulted in substantial gains for Hitler's party, making the NSDAP the largest party in the Reichstag, though they did not win an outright majority. After the second election (in November), the Nazis once again emerged as the largest party by far in the Reichstag, though their margins of victory were slightly narrower. To the siblings Klaus and Erika Man, who had founded the Pepper Grinder with actress Therese Giehse, it was time for desperate measures. The Manns' father, Nobel Prize-winning novelist Thomas Mann, described his children's efforts as "the swan song of the German republic." It was an accurate description.

Klaus Mann (1906–49) described the group's goal as presenting charmingly playful, but also the most bitter and passionate protest against the "brown [i.e., Nazi] infamy." In the audience at that Munich premiere was Wilhelm Frick, who was soon to become the national police chief. When mass arrests began after the Reichstag fire on February 27, 1933, the Manns quickly departed for Switzerland, where they began to perform in October at a hotel in Zurich. It was the first German-language "Exile Cabaret." Their practice of using the real names of leading Nazis in their satirical programs provoked the ire of the new Nazi government, which lodged protests with Swiss authorities. One of Erika Mann's most popular lines was, "Anybody who takes a shot at Goebbels will be hanged; anyone who shoots at Goering also gets hanged. But nobody shoots at Hitler!" Many local governments forbade such utterances, since most national governments in the 1930s sought to accommodate or even appease the Nazi regime. Meantime any guest who spoke about reality as they found it, and then wanted to be understood, was an unwelcome guest. Nazi sympathizers in Zurich needed no prompting to organize demonstrations against the group with the local Zurich government. Swiss

authorities meanwhile passed the "Pepper Grinder Law,"
which forbade any mention of political events or personalities
in any performance featuring foreigners. All members of the
Pepper Grinder troupe were foreigners, that is, non-Swiss. The
law had the desired effect of severely curtailing the group's
efforts by the end of 1933. Early in 1934 they embarked on
a tour throughout Switzerland, where Nazi sympathizers
attacked them physically, disrupted their performances with
stink bombs, or clogged toilets in venues where they attempted
to perform. Meantime the German Embassy in the Swiss
capital Berne lodged numerous protests against the group.
Those efforts likewise succeeded in decreased bookings. They
then went on tour to Holland, Belgium, Luxembourg, and
Czechoslovakia, where they received tumultuous welcomes
and a substantial amount of positive publicity. In the calendar
year of 1936, they completed 1,034 anti-Nazi performances
and seemed set for an American tour in 1937. Like most
cabaret performers in exile, they encountered resistance, legal
barriers, and other difficulties; from American authorities they
received merely indifference instead of opposition and non-
committal shrugs instead of outright resistance. The American
tour came to nothing, though Erika Mann later joined her
father in California.

Back in Zurich, Swiss native Walter Lesch (1898–1958)
formed the Cornichon cabaret with Otto Weissert (1903–69),
a German native but who had legal residence in Zurich. They
created programs in opposition to the Swiss organization
known as the *Frontenbewegung* (Front Movement), which
shared many of the views the Nazis espoused. Lesch and
Weissert's approach gradually attracted anti-Nazis. Lesch's
motto was "the humorist who remains a moralist soon becomes
a buffoon and a merchandiser."[12] Lesch and Weissert made a
special target of their satire the restrictive immigration policy
of the Swiss government. They also attacked the numerous
forms of unofficial antisemitism in Switzerland, along with
what they termed "well-established" Swiss tendencies toward
smugness, apathy, and cowardly non-interference in the

policies of Nazi Germany. The result was a hailstorm of protest from both Swiss citizens and the Nazi government, but Lesch refused all demands to remove objectionable material from the group's sketches and the lyrics of several songs. In response to a Zurich police inquiry about a song that compared Hitler favorably to the Pied Piper of Hamelin, Lesch replied, "If you forbid us the artistic freedom of indirect utterance of opinion (by means of artistic characterization), then you forbid us our essential effectiveness, which is an instrument of defending our country." The police withdrew their objections.

6

Cabaret in a Media-Driven Age

Aftermath

The Nazi attempt to use cabaret as a function of political propaganda was a small yet integral part of the regime's practice of terror, violence, cultural regeneration, and wholesale murder. By war's end, many believed that cabaret was nothing more than a corpse, never to be revived. Historical venues where cabaret had flourished lay in ruins. Artists who had somehow attempted to preserve it through the war years often found themselves in "displaced persons" confinement until such time as Allied troops could identify and release them. Cabaret nonetheless began a slow resurgence in the late summer of 1945, when occupation authorities attempted to bring the economic chaos of war under control. Among the first to attempt a resumption of cabaret performances were those who had largely tolerated or at times fully supported the regime, but who now found themselves destitute. Rudolf Schündler (1906–88) had appeared regularly with the Kabarett der Komiker (Kadeko) during the Nazi years, and he was among the first to obtain permission from the American occupation authorities in Bavaria to open a cabaret called the *Schaubude* (Show Shack) in Munich. The venue opened

for business in August 1945 in a newly repaired space at the
Munich Kammerspiele in the Maximillian Strasse. Six months
later, Schündler's group moved to a more permanent venue in
Munich, namely the Catholic Journeyman's Club in Reitmor
Strasse. There they did songs with lyrics by various writers
who had made names for themselves during the Weimar period
and who had survived the Nazi years. In 1948, however, a
currency reform went into effect in the Western zones of
occupation, and the new Deutsche Mark inadvertently forced
the Show Shack and most other cabarets into insolvency.[1]

Before the currency reform took effect, the Show Shack
premiered the first significant song of postwar cabaret,
Kästner's "Marschlied 45" (Marching Song 1945), to music
by Edmund Nick. "In the last three weeks," the lyrics say,
"I slogged through woods and field, my shirt so ripped and
torn, my wounds cannot be healed. A rucksack is my closet …
No home to go back to, no relatives to visit. It's nothing but
the Decline of the West—or is it?" The refrain concludes:
"Left, two, three four, left, two three—the past has passed,
and everything just smolders. Left, two, three, four, left, two,
three—but I've got my head still perched atop my shoulders."
Ursula Herking (1912–74) performed the song, and it helped
re-establish her career after the war. She had appeared in fifteen
films during the Nazi years and had been active in Werner
Finck's Catatacombs cabaret in Berlin and its successor, the
Cryptid Worm. When the Cryptid Worm closed, she worked
in the Berlin Kadeko until Goebbels ordered all performance
venues closed in August 1944. Exactly one year later she
was in Munich working with composer Nick, whose cabaret
career stretched all the way back to the early 1920s, when he
composed "I'm Bumbling Around with the Bees" for Blandine
Ebinger. During the Nazi years he wrote several popular
operettas along with musical scores for films.

With "Marching Song 1945" Herking became the
leading *diseuse* of the Show Shack and Kästner its leading
sketch writer and lyricist. Many hoped he might become
a stalwart of a hoped-for "cabaret of conscience" in the

spirit of "Never Again!" during the late 1940s.[2] During
the later 1940s and early 1950s, however, Kästner found
himself in an unaccustomed situation of affluence, thanks
to the royalties from his children's novel *Emil and the
Detectives*, which he had written in 1928. It had been
translated into several languages and after the war he
was allowed to collect overseas royalties in American and
British currencies.[3] He wrote other children's fiction in the
immediate postwar period, including the novel *Das doppelte
Lottchen* (Lottie and Lisa) which he adapted for a prize-
winning and highly lucrative film in 1950. For cabaret,
he created encounters among character types he had
encountered on the streets, most of them burned out in the
war and merely trying to survive. They included the ethnic
German woman whom nobody wants to help; the black
market operator who has something to offer everybody; the
politician, full of empty phrases and promises; and finally
a poet, moaning and complaining that nobody ever listens
to poets. Yet Kästner could not quiet misgivings about his
decision to remain in Nazi Germany and embark on "inner
emigration," which was perceived somehow as self-serving.
He had attended book burnings to witness his own books
destroyed and himself denounced. In 1951, Kästner began
working with *Die kleine Freiheit* (Little Liberty) cabaret
in Munich, for which he wrote numerous condemnations
of tendencies in German life which, he believed, had made
the Nazi dictatorship possible. Among them he believed
was the lust for money, which the currency reform of 1948
abetted. The whole idea of *Wohlstand für alle* ("Prosperity
for Everybody") as an election rallying cry for the center-
right parties (the Christian Democratic Union and the
Christian Social Union) in the 1950s left Kästner somewhat
perplexed. What kind of "prosperity," he wondered, requires
Germans to work like maniacs, so that they can once again
overindulge themselves? They're buying clothes they'll wear
maybe once or twice, he noted, and more coal than they
needed to get through the winter. They buy furniture just so

they don't have to sit on empty grocery crates. His were anti-consumerist jeremiads, but among people who had suffered food shortages, inadequate clothing, and insufficient heat, his preachings had little impact.

In bombed-out Hamburg, composer Lotar Olias (1913–90) founded the Bonbonniere cabaret shortly after Christmas in 1945. Olias had been an active member of the Nazi Party, writing several songs for Party gatherings, including a march with the distasteful words "God bless our Führer and his mighty deeds, May he protect us from Jews and other lesser breeds." Olias had worked during the war as a pianist with a traveling soldier cabaret group called the *Knobelbecher* (Jackboots), but his work in Hamburg demanded his talents not only as a pianist and songwriter: he also functioned as a master of ceremonies and sketch writer. Olias' strong suit was composing songs that were melodic, superficial, and entertaining. They avoided any question of what had happened during the Nazi years. He offered no condemnation, and his audiences expected no excuses. By 1949, Olias made a comeback with hit songs on radio, film music, and musical comedies. In the 1950s and 1960s he had several songs that reached the top of the German hit parade, and his "You, You, You" became a popular ballad for the Ames Brothers on American charts in 1953. Olias' most successful hits in German were recorded by Freddy Quinn (Franz Eugen Helmut Manfred Nidl, 1931–), two of which were million-sellers.

After his military unit surrendered to American forces in Italy, Werner Finck returned with other prisoners of war to Bavaria, where he remained until 1946. In that year he appeared in various locales, but in 1947 he made his way to Zurich to lead the *Nebelhorn* (Fog Horn) cabaret. The next year found him in Stuttgart with a group called *Mausefalle* (The Mouse Trap), which later moved to Hamburg. In between he did a number of popular solo shows, a venture that took him to South America for a six-month tour. By the 1950s he concentrated on solo shows throughout the new Federal Republic, satirizing political developments, and founded his own political party, the "Radical Middle." In 1973, the Federal Republic bestowed upon Finck its highest civilian honor, the Federal Service Cross.

The Economic Miracle

The rapid recovery of the West German economy (called the *Wirtschaftswunder* or "economic miracle") began with the currency reform of 1948. That reform also prompted severe protests from the Soviet Union and the eventual blockade of Berlin. Some venues managed to stay open, among them the Kom(m)ödchen (a play on the words "comedy" [*Komodie*] and "chest of drawers" [*Kommode*]) in Düsseldorf. The first program of the group was titled "Positively against It," referring to the currency reform. The most significant impact on cabaret venues in the wake of the currency reform, however, was the increasing number of cabaret programs broadcast on radio. The new currency helped to stabilize government financing, and, since all broadcasting was state-owned, there was little to no commercial competition among broadcasters. There was, however, a competition for filling vast amounts of air-time on the numerous frequency assignments. Among the first cabaret groups to broadcast their programs were the Insulaner (the "Islanders," a nod to West Berlin's status as a democratic island in the middle of Soviet-controlled East Germany) on the RIAS (Radio in the American Sector) broadcaster in West Berlin. The Islanders' leader was Günter Neumann, who had worked with Werner Finck in the Katakombe in the early 1930s. Neumann's group adhered to a forceful anti-Communist protocol, which perhaps explained its popularity in East Berlin. It remained on the air until the erection of the Berlin Wall in 1961. By that time, Neumann stated, the world had reached a point of serious conflict no form of laughter could ameliorate.

Some critics deplored currency reform as the cause of dividing Germany into separate entities with completely different and antagonistic economic and political systems. Others believed that politicians in West Germany instituted economic reforms and promoted the economic miracle as means to limit the effectiveness of cabaret's becoming a moral witness to the atrocities of the Nazi period. Millions of West Germans accepted the policies of the new government and its constitution (the *Grundgesetz*, or Basic Law), which went into effect in 1949. Its basic provisions included inviolable rights of speech, assembly, and press freedoms. For the performing arts, and for cabaret in particular, the freedoms of speech and assembly were obviously important, but the determining factor in the content of most cabaret programs during the 1950s was economics. The average audience, as Volker Kühn has humorously noted, accepted their status as good boys and girls in the school of democracy. They had rolled up their sleeves to clean away the debris of horrors left by dictatorship, just as they worked to clean up the rubble and ashes left by Allied bombing raids. They were now ready to enjoy the fruits of their extensive labors by re-building the country; they dreamed of house and garden, and of garden paths in bloom. They also accepted the "new German credo," coined by the Düsseldorf troupe *Kom(m)ödchen*: "One bockwurst is good. Two bockwursts are better" (Kühn 1993: 123).

From the postwar period and the economic miracle years of the early 1950s through his retirement in 1963, West German Chancellor Konrad Adenauer (1876–1967) had a powerful influence on cabaret in West Germany. Even his physiognomy—the wrinkled old guy in his eighties who was everybody's grandpa—was an inspiration for every caricaturist in the country. He was the object of many cabaret routines—the chieftain of his tribe, his jolly smile always in place, always a wholesome target for ribbing. Adenauer had opposed the Nuremberg War Trials; he insisted upon the release of convicted war criminals; he terminated the "denazification" process throughout the country; he ignored pleas for reunification with the Eastern occupation zone because it would mean a neutral Germany. He insisted that

West Germany align itself with Western powers and arranged for West Germany's membership in the North Atlantic Treaty Organization. He recognized Israel as the logical representative of the Jewish people and arranged for billions in reparations to be paid to destitute Jews there. For these and other reasons, Adenauer became a controversial figure. There were several attempts by Jewish groups to assassinate him, but Adenauer was a blessing for cabaret, even though the currency reform he and Finance Minister Ludwig Erhard had devised placed hardships on many cabaret venues. The "economic miracle" slowly awakened some cabarets, which began to bestow a peculiar form of gratitude upon Adenauer. They criticized him, they protested against him, they mounted superficial, rhymed objections to him, and they had an enormous amount of fun at his expense—all of which made Adenauer ever more popular and electable among voters. He was re-elected for a fourth term as chancellor at age eighty-five.

Cabaret on the Airwaves

The key phrase that entered the general idiom by the mid-1950s was *Wir sind wieder wer* (We are somebody again), which the federal minister of economics Ludwig Erhard (1897–1977) had coined. The steady increase in German economic productivity provided collateral increases in tax revenues to state and local governments, both of which used such funds to establish public broadcasting facilities (while also subsidizing established cultural ventures such as museums, theaters, and orchestras, but not cabarets). One of the first to broadcast radio and television cabaret programs was the Bavarian Radio Network in Munich. Their broadcasts of the Munich *Lach-und Shiessgesellschaft* (*Laugh- and Shooting Society*) proved to be one of the most popular of all programs the network offered. By 1957, the group's programs went national, as several state and local stations around the country picked up the broadcast feed from Munich.

Also on the radio in Munich was the voice of Karl Valentin (1882–1948), who claimed that on the previous night his wife had eased his pain by "rubbing my ribs with rhubarb," and that the soil in Germany had become a softer place for corpses, since there was a shovel shortage. Broadcast authorities at Bavarian State Radio soon thereafter removed him from the airwaves. Dancer Valeska Gert (1892–1978) encountered similar problematic responses from audiences in the immediate postwar years. Upon her return to Berlin from New York in 1948, her rather grotesque version of a stereotypical female warden at a concentration camp did not go over well. By late June 1948, the blockade of West Berlin by Russian forces had caused a change in Berlin audiences. Provocations like Gert's tended to bring back "unpleasant memories" of terror and deprivation. Gert, along with performers at the Badewanne (the Bathtub), created recognizable specters with distinctly unpleasant associations in the minds of many audience members. Her performances of "Variations on Suicide" likewise failed to strike happy notes among patrons. The Bathtub lasted only six months before disbanding. In their place arose a more popular group in Berlin, *Die Stachelschweine* (The Porcupines).

The Porcupines' first program (in October of 1949) was titled "Everything Crazy Funny," and their admission policy was *ein Knopf pro Kopf* ("one button per head"). Cabaret performers personally cut off buttons from patrons' clothing as they entered the venue; the Porcupines' work gradually grew in popularity, even though they had to move their operations several times due to structural damage their various locales had suffered from bombing raids. The group also suffered artistically from ongoing personnel changes. By 1952, however, the quality of the group's work improved considerably with the addition of Wolfgang Neuss (1923–89).

Among the very best of cabaret performers in the postwar period, Neuss had a solo act he titled "The Neuss Testament," featuring a severely didactic orientation. Yet Neuss (see Figure 10) also published a handbill newspaper called *Neuss Deutschland*, which parodied so-called socialist practices

Figure 10 *Wolfgang Neuss, ca. 1958. ©United Archives GmbH/ Alamy Stock Photo.*

endorsed by the East German party organ *Neues Deutschland*. Because he parodied East Germany, West German authorities found his position constructive (Appignanesi 2004: 173). One of Neuss' most popular sketches was "Uncle Paul writes from the Black Sea," a fictive letter to relatives back in Germany. He makes fun of himself as a West German, claiming that among the East Germans (who occupy a camping place near his luxurious hotel) he is regarded as the Kaiser himself.

> When I'm in a good mood, I throw a Deutsche Mark coin onto the sand and there is such a scramble for it that I now have three servants at my beck and call. It's almost like it was when I was in the army, assigned to Paris back in 1940. Only more Slavic, because Poles and Czechs have now joined the East Germans.

Neuss had served five years in the German army during the Second World War, and he was awarded several medals for bravery. One was for losing the index finger on his left hand, which he later inferred was self-inflicted. The missing index finger did not hinder Neuss from creating another solo act he called "The Man with the Drum," using a large bass drum to accentuate the punch lines in many of his routines.

> In New York, they say, "Berlin is our problem child," and that's why they don't want to play with us. Man, if you've got a child you've got to play with him, beat the drum with him … But they let our blonde Hildegarde[4] on Broadway, where she wowed 'em. There they have the whole range of things to please the German soul, from Alraune[5] to Al Capone.

Several performers imitated Neuss' one-man drum-pounding routine, and the result was a kind of return to the early days in Montmarte, when Aristide Bruant took aim at various bourgeois targets, informing them they were no better than the various whores and pimps in the audience. In the case of Neuss and his imitators, the target was the "higher-ups" in West German government, whom he identified by name, their misdeeds in office, and the favors they handed out to their supporters.

"I'm thinking I'll have my ass blasted with Cuban sugar tomorrow," Neuss once confessed.

I don't really need it, but when you can afford something, why not? Yesterday Helga got a manicure. Only on her toes. Two art history students from Leipzig did it. Helga now has a completely different view of East Germany. Please excuse me for writing with a typewriter. But I traded three ball-point pens for a pound of caviar from Odessa. This is the way I imagine the reunification of Germany.

East Germany

Nobody in the 1970s realistically imagined that Germany would ever be reunited. Certainly the cabaret artists in East Germany did not. Peter Jelavich has accurately noted that East German cabaret's task was nearly impossible: to identify weaknesses of the socialist system, but never to impugn nor de-legitimize socialism itself. Cabaret artists were to "point out problems which they hoped their efforts would ameliorate" (Jelavich 2000: 164). The inherent paradox within such a situation was evident.

The troupes were supposed to employ satire, which is normally aimed at those in power. Cabarets were allowed to criticize shortfalls in the actual development of socialism, without attacking socialism's fundamental precepts. In principle, even that task should have given great leeway to cabaret. After all, the classic German conception of satire, voiced by generations of writers dating back to the eighteenth century, was to highlight the discrepancy between ideals and realities.

That notion continued to activate numerous satirists in the GDR, who genuinely believed in socialist principles. But those satirists saw that those principles were getting short shrift in the society they inhabited (Jelavich 2000: 165).

The postwar situation in East Germany was altogether different from what performers and audiences experienced in the West. The East German sector from the beginning fell under Soviet domination, which insisted that only German Communists, under the direction of Soviet leader Stalin, had resisted the Hitler dictatorship effectively. The East German government, when it came into being in 1949, began providing subsidies to cabaret (unlike the West German government), and its ruling Social Unity Party insisted that cabaret performers continue to work in the tradition of the agitprop movement of the early 1930s. That tradition included an insistence on social justice and a condemnation of capitalism. Performers accepted conditions the government stipulated, which included authorized supervision of all material for performance. The first cabaret of note in East Berlin was *Die Distel* (The Thistle), which declaimed, "We embrace the Socialist Unity Party, which is what basically differentiates us from cabarets in the West." In Leipzig the *Pfeffermühle* (Pepper Grinder) likewise followed the party line, though its director Conrad Reinhold had a different interpretation of that difference: in the East, he noted, cabaret is supposed to change everything but is not allowed to say anything. In the West, cabaret is supposed to say everything, but not allowed to change anything (Kühn 1993: 185).

Fat and Overfed

By the time Adenauer retired in 1963, some critics began to accuse cabarets of being fat, overfed, and self-satisfied. They made lots of money on television and, since all television in West Germany was state-controlled, they were analogous to East German state cabarets. Other critics derided them as upholstered lounges where scoffers congregated. West German politicians, however, began to enjoy seeing parodies of themselves on television. Some even made a special effort to be present in the audience when a televised version of themselves was subjected to ridicule or derision. Some critics dismissed a "congratulatory cabaret" as a perversion of what cabaret was supposed to be. Wasn't cabaret supposed to be a mild form of conspiracy? Wasn't there supposed to be a whiff of anarchism in the air at a cabaret performance? And what about provocation? "Who's getting provoked anyway?" asked one critic, himself highly provoked (Kühn 1993: 215). West Germans had fabulous cabaret on television. But some argued that it is hardly cabaret when a viewer can simply turn off the TV set and go to bed. Such estimations could, however, have described cabaret in Montmartre; once cabaret becomes popular, it runs the risk of becoming institutionalized. No less a figure than Aristide Bruant repeatedly told his adoring crowds to go screw themselves, realizing that he had no way of protecting himself from their veneration. It is a dilemma many performing artists experience, especially if they become identified with a particular anti-Establishment, anti-war, or any other accusatory political pose. Maintaining an adversarial stance over an extended period of time—especially if the public begins to appoint a popular adversary as their adumbrative public personality—becomes increasingly difficult.

The economic miracle was responsible for dulling what had been cabaret's scalpel, since in most cases it had never been a rapier or even a pocket knife. Thanks to the rapid recovery of the West German economy, cabaret's "edge" was becoming simply another diversion for hard-working but fatigued entertainment consumers. And those consumers were largely self-satisfied philistines, half-educated defenders of inherited values, many of which remained, in the postwar period, highly suspicious. Germans were becoming fat, not only at the waist, but also intellectually. Cabaret thus began to fuel suspicions among younger Germans about the economic miracle and the way West Germany was developing as a whole. Those who opposed the democratic, parliamentary system began to see cabaret as a "paid agent" of the "system." Exiles such as Friedrich Hollaender did not always find a warm welcome when they returned. He resumed work on "revuettes" in Munich and Hamburg through the 1950s and 1960s, but for many his work carried a distinct whiff of nostalgia. His appearances on television garnered a wide viewership, but he too seemed to have lost his "edge." Hollaender's erstwhile son-in-law Georg Kriesler (1922–2011) fared somewhat better, although his expertise lay in solo acts on the piano and a prolific output of songs he wrote for himself. Kreisler had attended high school in Hollywood (where he met Hollaender's daughter Phillene, whose mother was Blandine Ebinger). Like his father-in-law at the same age, Kreisler played piano on tours to entertain troops (American troops, in his case; he had enlisted in the American army in 1943). In 1955, Kreisler returned to Europe and began work in several venues, including the Porcupines in Berlin.

Kreisler's first base upon his return, however, was Vienna. There he began working with a group who called themselves The Nameless Ensemble. Their founders were Michael Kehlmann (1927–2005), Carl Merz (1906–79), and Helmut Qualtinger (1928–86), who had met as students and began performing together in 1948 as *Die Grimasse* (The Grimace). With them, cabaret veterans such as Paul Morgan and Roda Roda were active, but the most significant figure of the group was Qualtinger. Helmut Qualtinger had studied medicine and later became a part-time reporter. His first attempts at cabaret came to nothing, but when he began working with Kehlmann and Merz, he experienced popular appeal for the first time. The group went on tour and found appeal likewise among Austrian audiences generally; from 1952 until 1961 the group remained together as the Nameless—unnamed but eminently recognizable thanks to the outsized proportions of Qualtinger's immense girth and his triple chin. Qualtinger was also a gifted singer, but after 1961 he was best known for the character of Herr Karl. He and Merz created Herr Karl as a one-man show, and after premiering it on Austrian national television he became so closely identified with the character that it became his primary source of income during the 1960s and 1970s. Herr Karl was a grocery clerk with an astounding cache of information about twentieth-century Austrian history. He began the show with an imaginary conversation with a customer in the grocery store about the collapse of the Habsburg Empire, then moved on to the turbulence and chaos of the 1920s and 1930s. He recalled Germany's annexation of Austria in 1938, bringing fine detail to the character who was apparently ready to take advantage of any situation that came his way. By the time the Second World War was over and Austria was accorded neutral independence, Herr Karl is clearly taking financial advantage of every shortage, operating as a kind of black marketeer. The character that emerged was an unflattering reflection of the Austrian *Schieber*, a con-man, opportunist, and grafter. Qualtinger had hit a sensitive Austrian nerve in the creation of Herr Karl; many Austrians saw themselves in the portrait, and Qualtinger began to get death threats from individuals who believed his performance was actually an accusation. Qualtinger toured with the show throughout most of western Europe, and in 1963 he introduced "Mr. Karl" to New York audiences for a two-week sold-out run at the Barbizon Plaza Hotel Theatre.

In Basel, actor Alfred Rasser (1907–97) established a folksy character named Theophil Läppli with the group *Resslirytti Basel*, named for the Resslirytti Hotel, where the group performed. Later Rasser joined *Cornichon Basel*, taking the character Läppli with him. The character was a spoof on the smug Swiss type, though dim-witted and often unable to figure out what was going on around him. The type had much in common with "the Good Soldier Schweyk" from the 1921 novel by Jaroslav Hašek. Both Schweyk and Läppli were incompetent, but their incompetence became a form of anti-militarism. Rasser formed a dual act with Charles Ferdinand Vaucher (1902–72) which they called *Kaktus*, and his sketches

with Vaucher of Läppli proved so popular that they could fill
venues that seated over 1,000 patrons per night. In the 1950s,
Rasser completed several films with Läppli as the central
figure: *Läppli am Zoll* (1954), *HD-Soldat Läppli* (1959), and
Demokrat Läppli (1961).

This focus on the creation of a solo persona shows how
cabaret, centered on the *Vortragskünstler*, the "recitation
artist," gives birth to contemporary stand-up comedy. The
activity, the purpose, and the modus of both forms are identical.

The Revolt of the '68ers

By 1968, many cabaret performers began to define "freedom,"
"justice," and "equality" in terms of socialist ideals. The Little
Liberty group in Munich, for example, addressed problems
such as prisons, child welfare, housing, and medical care. Its
leader Dieter Uthoff wrote sketches that presented clichés about
social problems and then pretended to interview performers
playing social workers, governments bureaucrats, and doctors
to determine how a truly socialistic state would improve
those problems. The result was a "Documentary Cabaret," a
format which swept through several venues in West Germany,
presenting statistics in musical form, with monologues,
photographs, placards, and sketches that lent a vague form of
authenticity to social critique. Increasingly polemical, cabarets
became venues where performers and audiences could agree
on the necessity of wholesale social upheaval.

"Apo cabaret, not Opa's cabaret"[6] was the short-lived
catchphrase of the late 1960s and early 1970s. Previous cabaret
performers, writers, and creators had accepted the idea that a
crucial ingredient in any cabaret was laughter. Not the "68ers."
Left-wing students formed cabarets with programs of radical
preaching in mind. Ernst Bloch's utopian *The Principle of
Hope*, written while in American exile from the Nazis, became
sacred writ for many would-be revolutionaries.[7] Organizers

of the student cabaret *Das Bugelbrett* (The Ironing Board) in Heidelberg actually turned portions of it into sketches, one of them titled "Red is the Color of Hope!" Other student groups took Bloch's sentiments further, offering sketches such as "Stop Hoping for Red—Starting Acting Red!" Many used street protests to accelerate calls for a West German socialist republic, and the Nazi-influenced background of the new Chancellor Kurt-Georg Kiesinger[8] (1904–88) fueled calls for radical political change. Riots and demonstrations were prevalent on West German university campuses, and advocates of political cabaret tried to transform happenings on campuses into cabaret acts.

Audiences generally rejected such efforts. Cabaret remained a middlebrow activity, at which audiences mostly sought entertainment, or at least an hour or two of relief from the reports in German media about street demonstrations. Rumors of East German collusion with student revolutionaries did not spur attendance, either. The Berlin Reichskabarett was an exception, perhaps because their programs sported humorous titles like "The Guerilla Says Hi," "Everything Has its Limits," "With Culture in Our Hearts," and "Hey! Where's My Money?" This group was also noteworthy for its attention to children's audiences, and for them its programs were also funny but were rarely provocative. There were several discussions by the end of the 1960s about where West German cabaret was going and where it might end. Heirs wanted to distance themselves from their legacy; they were convinced that cabaret as they had come to know it could not continue.

At a 1968 cabaret conference in Essen, several attendees staged a demonstration in the streets, demanding a new direction for cabaret. The days of conventional cabaret were over, they concluded. They furthermore believed that cabaret could not stand idly by as the extra-parliamentary opposition confronted the Establishment. The conference revealed a split within cabaret devotees: one side steadfastly refused to make cabaret in West Germany resemble agitprop troupes of the early 1930s. The other side believed cabaret had an abstract duty to engage in contemporary politics. Neither side prevailed, as one observer later noted in a quote from Kurt Tucholsky: "Success 1, Influence zero."[9]

That dichotomy had always been there, and for several reasons. Some believed that cabaret was a kind of ghetto art form that had to force open doors if it was to be effective. Cabaret performers, after all, played before audiences who share similar sentiments, and that explained why those audiences tolerated or even enjoyed being harangued at times. The cabaret performer had no need to win over his or her audience. They're already convinced even before they arrive. So the performer often preached to the converted. What remained for the audience, then, was to take pleasure in the ways the performance adhered to formulaic lines of familiarity. The correct timing of a punch line, for example, the setup for an effective gag, or the rhyme schemes used in musical lyrics. Many 68ers had a different opinion. They saw cabaret as part of an overall strategy to change society, and to do so they had to change hearts and minds. They soon realized that jokes were not the most effective means of political agitation. One such group was Floh de Cologne.[10] They used projected photographs and recorded music, which usually included a heavy metal sound, pounding drumbeats, and a heavy application of political slogans to make their point, which ran something like "This society offers us the possibility of living without repression, but it enjoins us from employing that possibility. We thus have the right to flout this injunction" (Kühn 1993: 333). The time-honored practices of sketches, chansons, blackout-numbers, and the master of ceremonies were dead. Floh de Cologne urged audiences to "take action," which involved riding streetcars, buses, and subway trains without paying the fare. They also urged their audiences to move into empty buildings and establish "squatters' rights." They insisted that audience members practice "pre-marital sex or adultery." Smoking hashish was also highly recommended. So was staging demonstrations during rush hour, likewise the theft of basic

foodstuffs from grocery stores. "Cabaret?" someone asked.
"We really don't give a shit" was their answer. But where to
go from there?

Downhill

Cabaret's history of affecting political trends and influencing
the temper of the times was spotty at best. The 1970s in West
Germany were beset by home-grown terrorist attacks, political
assassinations, and increasing interference from East German
agents embedded within the West German government. Police
raids became commonplace in some cities, while some feared
that West Germany was becoming a police state. Few cabaret
artists found the situation funny. Some street demonstrators
and squatter groups attempted to perform cabaret, but
with little effect. Stand-up routines reflected the situation as
hopeless, but not serious: "What doesn't improve the situation
can't do much harm" was the lead-in to several routines. Some
cabaret routines took up the contemporary anxiety around
environmental despoliation. Others confronted the dilemma of
Third World poverty. Solo acts tended to concentrate on such
generalized phobias instead of day-to-day concerns in politics.
Lore Lorentz (1920–94) was one of the better stand-up
comediennes, having founded (with her husband Kay Lorenz)
the *Kom(m)ödchen* in Düsseldorf. Agitprop attempted a
comeback in some venues, but nobody seemed capable of using
humor to lament the stand-off between the Soviet Union and
the United States. Some cabaret-style shows on West German
television, such as *Notizen aus der Provinz* (News from the
Provinces) on the ZDF network and *Die Scheibenwäscher*
(The Windshield Washers) on ARD, tried to approach political
questions, but West German political reality did not lend itself
much to satire.

The East German situation stood in stark contrast to its West
German counterpart, even though East German politicians

offered luscious targets to any satirist who dared spoof them. And very few did. "Satire," as East German leader Walter Ulbricht (1893–1973) profoundly stated, "is what it must be." He and other Socialist Unity Party members (including his successor Erich Honnecker) favored licensing, subsidizing, manipulating, and censoring cabaret in East Germany; it thus became a kind of cultural workshop for manufacturing socialist humor. It did so as a subsidiary of the overall performance art industry, echoing official bulletins and trumpeting the wisdom of the Party's leadership. The Party, in turn, could not tolerate competition from an opinion-formation establishment beyond itself. So it built a tightrope and forced performers to "walk across the narrow gap between seeming accommodation and enciphered criticism" (Kühn 1993: 237).

As Peter Jelavich (2000: 164) has adroitly noted, East German troupes were allowed to criticize shortfalls in the actual development of socialism, but "without attacking socialism's fundamental precepts." In Tucholsky's phrase, the satirist is "an insulted idealist." Satire's duty as a subsidized art form was to remain utopian, stressing that the ideal was just over the horizon, despite the yawning gap between today and tomorrow, between reality and the ideal (in *Der Spiegel* 1966: 193). The collapse of the East German regime in November 1989 may have been too momentous for cabaret to handle. Nobody had even imagined such a turnabout in German politics. It took a while for cabaret to catch its breath and gather it all in.

Televised Cabaret

The prevailing problem with televised cabaret was the tendency of viewers simply to switch channels when things got boring, or to shut off the TV altogether and go to bed. In France, televised puppet cabaret flourished. *Les Arènes de l'info* (The News Arena) began in the late 1980s as a kind of weekly news review with hilarious results; similarly in Britain there was *Spitting Image*. But these are particular cases. As a whole, cabaret, the weed that had somehow grown up through cracks in the cultural asphalt, became by the 1960s a delivery service for the television industry (Kühn 1993: 365). On television, acts configured as "entertainment cabaret" suddenly appeared, then withered, and for all intents and purposes disappeared back into the asphalt.

Some German cabaret ensembles attempted on television to interpose politics into their entertainment routines. The aforementioned Lore Lorentz, active with the *Kom(m)ödchen* in Düsseldorf, began broadcasting from Hamburg on the Northwest German Network. In the same year Tatjana Seiss and Günter Neumann of the Islanders troupe began broadcasting from Berlin. A year later Wolfgang Gruner and Wolfgang Herbst from the *Stachelschwein* group began their broadcasts from Berlin broadcasts studios. By the mid-1950s, camera crews began to set up live transmissions from cabaret venues themselves. What they wanted, according to Friedrich Luft, was to capture "the original whiff and aroma of live performance" (Luft 1957: 52; also Hicketier 1998: 147).

Political cabaret traditionally took as its task the use of satire, irony, and hyperbole to goad or at least urge audiences into thinking about political structures and social change. Cabaret performers were expected to provide an impulse for social transformation. There was, however, considerable doubt concerning that self-assigned mission and thus cabaret's impact came into question. Viewers could see on the screen the presence of the powerful seated within a cabaret venue. They watched as the powerful laughed along with the audience at jokes made at their expense. They (the powerful) seemed thoroughly and honestly to be enjoying themselves—all the while giving little thought to instigating political or social change.

Cabaret on TV served another function. It ultimately presented an "elevated form" of political discourse, aimed at a well-educated, politically interested audience. It derived its existence from the fact that viewers could understand and appreciate innuendos, out of which emerged unexpected or unanticipated punch lines, jokes, or phrases. Cabaret had an "escape valve" function. Viewers could furthermore enjoy such wordplay, because they knew that it provoked few repercussions. There were, however, some instances of satirical bites, but as a whole cabaret's humor on television was "consensual humor," according to critic Volker Lilienthal (2003: 133).

Consensual humor was critical to the emergence of cabaret done purely for the sake of entertainment, a format that began to dominate television in Europe and America by the 1970s. Entertainment cabaret had its origins in the variety shows of radio broadcasting. Such broadcasts featured entertainment in small dosages, similar to cabaret's sketch routines consisting of skits and musical offerings, along with ironic commentary on everyday occurrences and general spoofing of cultural phenomena. A good example of a radio show with such formal characteristics in the United States was *The Jack Benny Program*, which began on radio in 1934 and switched to network television in 1950; it remained there, its radio format largely intact, until 1965. Meantime several other shows with similar formats developed, among them *That Was the Week That Was* on the British Broadcasting Corporation, which was far more political in its approach. *The Smothers Brothers Comedy Hour* in the United States likewise used pointed satire to pillory certain politicians, but like *That Was the Week That Was*, it lasted only two years. The variety format that has lasted longest has been *Saturday Night Live* in the United States, which began in 1975 and remains a fixture on national network television. The German version of *Saturday Night Live* was *Samstag Nacht*, which ran from 1993 to 1998 on the RTL network, following the format of the American show. It had very little in the way of intellectual exercise, or any intellectual appeal whatsoever. Like the American show, the German version presented in rapid order a series of disconnected skits, called "flow of comedy" in German, most of which had only nonsense to connect them.

Nonsense began to assume a larger and more predominant representation through the remainder of the twentieth century, which set off alarms in the minds of some critics. In the UK, *Monty Python's Flying Circus* captured a politically knowledgeable audience, though many of the sketches were exercises in the avoidance of substance or meaning. In West Germany, *Insterburg und Co.* followed a similar pattern, namely "the art of advanced bullshit" (*die Kunst des höheren Blödsinns*). Few sketches lasted longer than a minute, and the emphasis was on the rapid tempo at which those sketches followed each other, coupled with a diffident acceptance of the bizarre as completely normal. Several solo acts followed the popular precedent of nonsense, including that of Didi Hallervorden and especially of Otto Waalkes. For them and many others, laughter became "a kind of intellectual exercise" or perhaps a kind of "therapeutical substitute for intellectuals ... who longed for meaning-free rituals" (Bolz 1997; also Türcke 1998).

Thus cabaret, the form that grew through the cracks in the cultural pavement, with its makeshift venues and insults to the audience, found itself eventually in the expensive environment of the TV studio playing safely into the hands of an audience who wanted harmless entertainment.

NOTES

Introduction

1 Fröbe is best known to American and British audiences as "Gert Frobe," the eponymous anti-hero of the 1964 James Bond thriller *Goldfinger*.

2 The "Salzburg Bull" is a 500-year-old barrel organ, said to be the world's oldest automatic musical instrument. A human operator plays the instrument by turning one of its two barrels, on which musical craftsmen hammered pegs and rods. When a barrel turns, the pegs and rods intermittently open forced-air vents beneath the pipes to create bellowing tones in harmony with one another. What this instrument has in common with cabaret performance remains somewhat mysterious.

Chapter 1

1 The first French aperitif was Dubonnet, whose 1846 mixture of dry red wine mixed with quinine, herbs, and spices became a traditional pre-dinner drink. In 1805, the Swiss distiller Henri Pernod opened his French distillery, producing absinthe, a strongly alcoholic anise-flavored liquor. Absinthe was also popular in cabarets and taverns, though its use was considered somewhat declassé. The French government banned absinthe in 1915.

2 French courts recognized in 1850 the rights of music composers, and in 1851 a professional union called the Société des auteurs, compositeurs et éditeurs de musique (SACEM) became the authorized agency to collect royalties for published songs. SACEM initially had 350 members, and it still functions to this day. See https://societe.sacem.fr/en/history.

3   Like Montmartre, Ménilmontant, Bantignolles, and other
     districts, Belleville was an outlying suburb of Paris until its
     annexation in 1860.

Chapter 2

1   Some critics have metaphorically pitted Oskar Panizza (1853–
     1921) against his contemporary Oscar Wilde (1854–1900)
     in a contest for degeneracy. Panizza was the author of *Das
     Liebekonzil* in 1894, a comedy about the first documented
     outbreak of syphilis in Europe. The Bavarian Justice Ministry
     in Munich charged him with ninety-three counts of blasphemy
     in 1900 and convicted him on all of them, sentencing him to a
     year at hard labor in a penitentiary in Amberg. He never fully
     recovered from his year in prison and a court declared him
     insane in 1905.

2   *Tingel-Tangel* is best translated into English as "honky-tonk,"
     though the term "honky" has racial connotations absent in
     German usage. A good example of a German *Tingel-Tangel* is
     the place where Marlene Dietrich as Lola-Lola performs in the
     1931 film *The Blue Angel*: a bar with no bourgeois aspirations
     to respectability.

3   Contributing to the craze was the rise of tourism. Hotel
     occupancy rates soared at the beginning of the new century,
     with estimates of over a million visitors to Berlin each year.
     Like other Western European cities even at the end of the
     nineteenth century, Berlin had become a "tourist attraction,"
     a development which helped spur cabaret attendance first
     in Paris, and soon thereafter in Berlin. Police relaxation of
     normal morality codes and censorship rules in deference to
     international visitors also helped. See Fritzsche 1996: 66.

4   Bernauer's biggest hit during this period was probably "Wie
     einst im Mai" (One Upon a Time in May), which he wrote with
     Rudolf Schanzer. Walter and Willi Kollo later adapted it as an
     operetta, using their script as the libretto. The operetta survived
     two wars, the Weimar Republic's collapse, and the Hitler years,
     so beloved was it by all manner of audiences.

5   The founders of the Vienna Secession movement (1897)
    included Hoffmann, Klimt, Moser, and about forty others
    whose goal of renewing the decorative arts resembled the
    British Arts and Craft Movement. Its dissimilarity was its intent
    to "secede" from the powerful Vienna Academy of the Arts and
    other quasi-official art institutions in Vienna. Its most famous
    exhibition was in 1902, the "Beethoven Exhibition," for which
    Klimt composed a monumental "Beethoven Frieze" (covering
    784 square feet). The Frieze and its effect on viewers at the
    Exhibition can be seen in the 2019 ÖRF (Austrian Television
    Network) production *Vienna Blood* directed by Umut Dag.

Chapter 3

1   A replica of this machine is on display at the Berlin Musical
    Instrument Museum, located in the Ben-Gurion Strasse.

2   James J. Morton (1861–1938) was vaudeville's first Master
    of Ceremonies. He was a monologist who could segue into
    introducing other acts. Most vaudeville shows introduced acts
    with title cards that had the act's name written on it.

Chapter 4

1   Waldoff (with composer Kollo at the piano) performed the
    song almost every night for the next two years. They formed
    a lifelong friendship, writing and performing dozens of songs
    over the years, including one of her biggest hits "Ach Jott, was
    sind die Männer dumm" ("Oh God, Men Are So Stupid!"). In
    1923, Kollo began working with his nineteen-year-old son Willi,
    and their work together culminated in the 1933 production
    of the "comedy with songs" *Lieber Reich, aber Glücklich*
    (Preferably Rich, but Happy) by Franz Arnold and Ernst Bach,
    and in 1935 with *Das ist Berlin wie's weint, Berlin wie's lacht*
    (Berlin: its Tears and its Laughter). The music sounds a little
    like the early Jerome Kern.

2   Florenz Ziegfeld (1867–1932) staged his Follies mostly at the
    New Amsterdam Theatre on West 42nd Street until 1927;
    he thereafter staged them at his own property, the Ziegfeld
    Theatre at 1341 Sixth Ave. The Shubert Brothers staged
    their extravaganzas at the Winter Garden Theatre at 1634
    Broadway.

3   Wilhelm Bendow (Wilhelm Emil Bodon, 1884–1950) made his
    first cabaret appearance in 1919 at Hesterberg's Wilde Bühne
    venue. His speciality was the effeminate homosexual, whose
    voice flutterings and "prissy exterior" turned everything he
    did into a double-entendre. "Moon-faced, nasal-voiced and
    bespectacled, he delivered his commentary in a languorous
    sing-song that was the oral equivalent of a limp-wrist." He
    was also a cross-dressing sensation, though not what we
    might term today a "drag queen." He appeared in male and
    female costumes simultaneously, for example, in "Zeppelin
    1000 on Mars." According to Mel Gordon (in *Voluptuous
    Panic*) he enjoyed a wide following among Nazi government
    officials, opening his own venue called Bendow's Buntes Bühne
    in 1932 and continued for another year during the Hitler
    dictatorship.

4   Paul Morgan (Paul Morgenstern, 1886–1938) was one of the
    busiest emcees in the Weimar period at several different venues:
    cabarets, varietés, and revues. He escaped Berlin after the Nazi
    elections in 1933 and headed back to his native Vienna. But
    there, soon after the German annexation of Austria, he was
    arrested and sent first to the Dachau concentration camp and
    later to Buchenwald, where he died.

5   For his revues at the Winter Garden Theatre in New York,
    Shubert had a runway constructed that ran through the
    audience, on which his women made their entrances. Critics
    later dubbed that runway "the bridge of thighs."

6   Among the many idealized "American girls" whom Ziegfeld
    presented, and who later became stars on stage and in films
    were Marion Davies (1897–1961), Paulette Goddard (1910–
    80), Jeanne Eagels (1890–1929), Barbara Stanwyck (1907–90),
    and Louise Brooks (1906–85).

Chapter 5

1   Jannings' Oscar was the first Academy Award ever given to
     an actor, and he won it for two films: *The Way of All Flesh*
     (1927) and *The Last Command* (1928, also directed by von
     Sternberg).

2   Lerner later became, like Hollaender, a composer of film music,
     but his best-known musical creation was for Popeye cartoons.
     His "I'm Popeye the Sailor Man" theme song remains familiar
     today in numerous soundtracks for television and video games.

3   Frank Loesser (1910–69) was like Rudolf Nelson, Irving Berlin,
     and Hollaender himself in that he had no formal education
     in musical composition nor in writing lyrics. He nevertheless
     composed several Broadway hit musicals, among them *Guys
     and Dolls* (1950), *The Most Happy Fella* (1956), and *How to
     Succeed in Business without Really Trying* (1961).

4   The name "Kuhfort" was a play on the word "Kurort," the
     name in German which designates the presence of thermal
     springs, herbal mud, mineral drinking water, and other curative
     attractions, sometimes called spas. German medical culture has
     long advocated "taking the cure" in spas, which often have the
     term "Bad" ("bath") in their names.

5   "Blood and soil" (*Blut und Boden*) was a widely used locution
     within National Socialist ideology. Its origins probably derived
     from Oswald Spengler's 1922 volume *Der Untergang des
     Abendlandes* (*The Decline of the West*), but its place in policy
     platforms of National Socialist electoral campaigns came from
     the Argentine-German Ricardo Walther Darré (1895–1953),
     a prolific author on agrarian topics. His *Neuadel aus Blut
     und Boden* (*The New Aristocracy of Blood and Soil*) in 1930
     became popular among the Nazi readership, while Darré
     himself became Reich Minister for Nutrition and Agriculture in
     July 1933.

6   According to the Reich Citizenship Law, which included
     several corollaries, titles, and decrees, the only German citizens
     entitled to civil protections were those of "Aryan" ancestry.
     The law also defined who was a Jew. The former legal status of
     Jews (established in 1871) stipulated that Jews were members

of a religious or cultural community; the Nuremberg Laws, however, defined Jews as a race.

7   *Das schwarze Korps* was the official newspaper of the Schutzstaffel (protective squad), known colloquially as the "SS." The SS began as a paramilitary organization, but became one of the most feared and powerful units of terror throughout Germany and German-occupied countries.

8   Strength through Joy was the Nazi Party's leisure-time organization and became the most popular agency within the Nazi regime. It provided not only discount tickets to cabarets, theaters, symphony concerts, and art exhibitions; it also organized affordable ocean cruises and vacations for workers, along with ski trips for them to numerous Alpine destinations in Bavaria and Austria. One of its major fiascoes was the "Volkswagen Project," which was supposed to help workers buy their own cars. Though workers placed large deposits with the organization to receive a Volkswagen, not a single vehicle was ever delivered, and no depositor received a refund.

9   The Deutsche Arbeitsfront (DAF) boasted 5.3 million members in July of 1933, 16 million in 1934, and 25 million in late 1942, by which time the DAF had become the largest organization in the entire Nazi state.

10 Robert Ley (1890–1945) was one of many well-educated Nazis (he had an earned doctorate from the University of Münster in chemistry); Goebbels was another. He held a doctorate on "Wilhelm von Schütz as Dramatist" from the University of Heidelberg. Ley, however, was one of the few Nazi leaders who publicly advocated the annihilation of Jewry in Europe.

11 http://www.bbc.com/culture/story/20190829-how-britain-fought-hitler-with-humor

12 See http://tls.theaterwissenschaft.ch/wiki/WalterLesch

Chapter 6

1   In order to strengthen German economic recovery, the French occupiers joined the Americans and British in replacing the

former Reichsmark currency with the new Deutsche Mark in June 1948.

2   "Niemals wieder!" (Never again!) became a well-worn catchphrase in the immediate postwar period. Other words that became politicized clichés included *Aufbau* (rebuilding), *Entnazifizierung* (de-Nazification), and *Stunde Null* (zero hour).

3   Several film adaptations of *Emil and the Detectives* have appeared, the first in 1931 (directed by Billy Wilder).

4   Hildegarde Knef (1925–2002), known as Hildegarde Neff in *Silk Stockings*, a Cole Porter musical based on the 1939 Ernst Lubitsch film (with screenplay by Billy Wilder) titled *Ninotchka*. The show ran for 478 performances.

5   In the 1928 film *Alraune* (directed by Henrik Galeen) a mad scientist inseminates a prostitute with the semen of a hanged man. She gives birth to Alraune, who becomes a beautiful woman genetically programmed to kill every man who falls in love with her. Playing a supporting role in the film was the cabaret performer Valeska Gert. Hildegarde Knef played the role of Alraune in a 1952 film before coming to New York.

6   *Apo* in popular jargon meant *Ausserparliamentarische Opposition* (extra-parliamentary opposition), a protest movement which attracted a large following among West German university students; *Opa* is a colloquial German term meaning "grandpa."

7   The original title of Bloch's (1885–1977) three-volume *Das Prinzip Hoffnung* (1938–47) was supposed to be "The Dreams of a Better Life." He revised it substantially during the 1950s at the University of Leipzig, where he became a professor in 1949. East German authorities suppressed its publication, largely because his visions of utopia did not accord with theirs. The East German government forced him out of his position at the university, even while awarding him several prizes for his work.

8   Kiesinger had been a long-standing member of the Nazi Party, but fellow party members denounced him in 1944 for impeding the deportation of Jews and for espousing "defeatism."

9   "What makes me uneasy about my work is its influence. Does it have any? I'm not talking about success. That's not my

concern. I mean, it sometimes seems so pointless. You sit there and write, and work—and what happens in the larger scheme of things? It's really depressing." See Tucholsky 1983b: 255.

10   In the long-standing tradition of puns in cabaret, *Floh de Cologne* was a play on Eau de Cologne, a well-known perfume. Meantime the word *Floh* in German meant "flea."

REFERENCES

Abrams, Lynn (1988), "Prostitutes in Imperial Germany 1870–1918: Working Girls or Social Outcasts?," in *The German Underworld: Deviants and Outcasts in German History*, ed. Richard Evans. New York: Routledge, 189–209.

Appignanesi, Lisa (2004), *The Cabaret*. New Haven: Yale University Press.

Ball, Hugo (1927), *Die Flucht aus der Zeit*. Munich: Duncker und Humblodt.

Bauschinger, Sigrid (2000), *Literarisches und politisches Kabarett von 1901 bis 1999*. Tübingen: Francke.

Bayerdörfer, Hans-Peter and Karl Otto Conrady, eds. (1978), *Literatur und Theater im wilhelminischen Zeitalter*. Tübingen: Niemayer.

Berlin am Morgen (1929), "Die Katakombe," October 20.

Bernauer, Rudolf (1955), *Das Theater meines Lebens*. Berlin: Blanvalet.

Bierbaum, Otto Julius (1900), *Deutsche Chansons*. Berlin: Schuster und Loeffler.

Bierbaum, Otto Julius (1901), *Stilpe, ein Roman aus der Froschperspektive*. Berlin: Schuster und Loeffler.

Bloch, Ernst (1962), *Erbschaft dieser Zeit*. Frankfurt am Main: Suhrkamp.

Bolz, Norbert (1997), "Der Sinn im Unsinn: die Lust am bedeutungsfreien Ritual," *Die Zeit*, May 30.

Brecht, Bertolt (1957), *Brecht on Theatre*, ed. John Willet. New York: Hill and Wang.

Bruant, Aristide (1972), *Aristide Bruant par lui-même*. Paris: Seghers.

Bruant, Aristide and Léon de Bercy (1905), *L'argot au XXc siècle: Dictionnaire français-argot*. Paris: Flammarion.

Budzinski, Klaus and Reinhard Hippen (1996), *Metzler Kabarett Lexikon*. Stuttgart/Weimar: Metzler.

Burt, Ramsay (1995), "Zurich Dada Conference," *Dance Research Journal* 27 (1): 65–7.

Carossa, Hans (1928), *Eine Kindheit: Verwandlung einer Jugend*. Leipzig: Insel.

Der Spiegel (1966), "Katakombe: Überwachung angebracht," April 4, 168.

Ewers, Hanns Heinz (1904), *Das Cabaret*. Berlin: Schuster und Loeffler.

Falckenberg, Otto (1944), *Mein Leben, mein Theater*. Munich: Zinnen.

Finck, Werner (1966), *Witz als Schicksal, Schicksal als Witz*. Hamburg: von Schröder.

Forcht, Georg (2009), *Frank Wedekind und die Anfänge des deutschen Kabaretts*. Freiburg i. Br.: Centaur.

Friedell, Egon (1985), *Meine Doppelseele: taktlose Bermerkungen zum Theater*, ed. Heribert Illig, Vienna: Löcker.

Fritzsche, Peter (1996), *Reading Berlin 1900*. Cambridge, MA: Harvard University Press.

Fröhlich, Elke, ed. (1998), *Die Tagebücher von Joseph Goebbels*, 6 Vols. Munich: Saur.

Goebbels, Joseph (1977), *Tagebücher*, Hamburg: Hoffmann und Campe.

Gordon, Mel and Sebastian Droste (2006), *The Seven Addictions and Five Professions of Anita Berber, Weimar Berlin's Priestess of Depravity*. Los Angeles: Feral House.

Greul, Heinz (1967), *Bretter, die die Zeit bedeuten: die Kulturgeschichte des Kabaretts*. Cologne: Kiepenheuer und Witsch.

Gumppenberg, Hanns von (1929), *Lebenserinnerungen*. Berlin: Eigenbrödler.

Gyárfás, Dezső (1920), *Orfeum: Egy színész élete* (The Life of an Actor). Budapest: n.p., http://mek.oszk.hu/02100/02139/html/sz09/11.html

Hake, Sabine (2017), *The Proletarian Dream: Socialism, Culture, and Emotion in Germany, 1863–1933*. Berlin: De Gruyter.

Ham, Jennifer (2000), "Galgenlieder und Tantenmörder: Criminal Acts as Entertainment in Early Munich Cabaret," in *Die freche Muse: literarisches und politisches Kabarett von 1901 bis 1999*, ed. Sigrid Bauschinger. Tübingen: Francke, 39–58.

Haustedt, Birgit (2013), *Die wilden Jahre in Berlin: eine Klatsch- und Kulturgeschichte der Frauen*. Berlin: Ebersbach.

Heap, Chad (2009), *Slumming in American Nightlife 1885–1940*.
     Chicago: University of Chicago Press.

Heinrich-Jost, Ingrid (1982), *Hungrige Pegasusse: Anfänge des
     deutschen Kababretts in Berlin*. Berlin: Adolf-Glassbrenner-
     Gesellschaft.

Hennessey, Thomas J. (1994), *From Jazz to Swing: African American
     Jazz Musicians and Their Music 1890–1935*. Detroit: Wayne
     State University Press.

Henningsen, Jürgen (1967), *Theorie des Kabaretts*. Ratingen: Henn.

Hérail, René-James and Edwin A. Lovatt (1984), *Dictionary of
     Modern Colloquial French*. London: Routledge.

Hermann, Regine (1981), "Theaterarbeit im französischen Exil," in
     Exil in Frankreich, ed. Dieter Schiller. Leipzig: Philipp Reclam
     jun., 272–302.

Hicketier, Knut (1998), *Geschichte des Fernsehens*. Stuttgart:
     Weimar.

Household Words (1857), "French Tavern Life," Vol. XVI, July–
     December.

Hughes, Erika (2009), "Art and Illegality on the Weimar Stage,"
     Journal of European Studies 39 (3): 320–35.

Huelsenbeck, Richard (1974), *Memoirs of a Dada Drummer*.
     New York: Viking.

Jelavich, Peter (1990), "Modernity, Civic Identity, and Metropolitan
     Entertainment," in *Berlin: Culture and Metropolis*, ed. Charles W.
     Haxtahusen. Minnepaolis: University of Minnesota Press, 95–110.

Jelavich, Peter (1993), *Berlin Cabaret*. Cambridge, MA: Harvard
     University Press.

Jelavich, Peter (2000), "Satire under Socialism: Cabaret in the
     German Democratic Republic," in *Die freche Muse: literarisches
     und politisches Kabarett von 1901 bis 1999*, ed. Sigrid
     Bauschinger. Tübingen: Francke, 164–78.

Jansen, Wolfgang (1987), *Glanzrevuen der Zwanziger Jahren*. Berlin:
     Hentrich.

Klabund (1916), "Cabaret Voltaire," *Berliner Tageblatt*, February 7.

Klabund (1927), *Die Harfenjule: neue Zeit-, Streit- und
     Leidgedichte*. Berlin: Schmiede.

Klossowski, Erich (1903), *Die Maler von Montmartre*. Berlin: Bard.

Koss, Juliet (1996), "Hooked on Kracauer," *Assemblage* 31: 80–9.

Kosztolányi, Dezső (2009), quoted in "The Pest Cabarets," https://
     sites.google.com/site/tattoomaniatattoo/kapirgak/the-pest-
     cabarets-1

Kothes, Franz-Peter (1977), *Die theatralische Revue in Berlin und Wien, 1900–1938*. Wilhelmshaven: Heinrichshofen.

Kracauer, Siegfried (1977), "Kult der Zerstreuung," in *Das Ormament der Masse: Essays*. Frankfurt am Main: Suhrkamp, 314–15.

Kuckhoff, Adam (1928), "Größe und Niedergang der Revue," *Die Volksbühne* 3 (1): 5.

Kühn, Volker (1987), *Donnerwetter–tadellos! Kabarett zur Kaiserzeit, 1900–1918*. Weinheim: Quadriga.

Kühn, Volker (1988), *Hoppla, wir beben: Kabarett einer gewissen Republik, 1918–1933*. Weinheim: Quadriga.

Kühn, Volker (1993), *Kleinkunststücke: Wir sind so frei: Kabarett in Restdeutschland, 1945–1970*. Weinheim: Quadriga.

Kutscher, Arthur (1927), *Frank Wedekind: sein Leben und seine Werke*, Vol. II. Munich: Müller.

Lareau, Alan (1995), *The Wild Stage: Literary Cabarets of the Weimar Republic*. Columbia, SC: Camden House.

Lareau, Alan (2000), "Du hast ja eine Träne im Knopfloch," in *Die freche Muse: literarisches und politisches Kabarett von 1901 bis 1999*, ed. Sigrid Bauschinger. Tübingen: Francke, 111–29.

Large, David (1998), *Hitlers München: Aufstieg und Fall der Hauptstadt der Bewegung*. Munich: Beck.

Lee, Jennifer (2009), "When 'Slumming' Was the Thing to Do," *New York Times*, July 6.

Lilienthal, Volker (2003), "Frosch im Mixer," in *Humor in den Medien*, ed. Walter Klinger. Baden-Baden: Nomos, 7–10.

Ludwig, Volker (1966), "Von der Schwierigkeit, sein Publikum zu ärgern," *Essener Jugend* II: 7.

Luft, Friedrich (1957), "Das Wort hat: der Kritiker," *Hör zu* 15: 52.

Marx, Karl and Friedrich Engels (1848), *Manifest der kommunistichen Partei*. London: Burghard.

McNally, Joanne (2000), "The Changing Discourses of German Cabaret in Response to National Socialism between 1929 and1935," in *Die freche Muse: literarisches und politisches Kabarett von 1901 bis 1999*, ed. Sigrid Bauschinger. Tübingen: Francke, 145–61.

Murger, Henri (1888), Preface to *The Bohemians of the Latin Quarter*. London: Vizetelly.

O'Neal, Michael J. (2006), *America in the 1920s*. New York: Facts on File.

Osofsky, Gilbert (1966), *Harlem: The Making of a Ghetto, Negro New York, 1890–1930*. New York: Harper & Row.

Panizza, Oskar (1898), "Der Klassizismus und das Eindringen des Variété," *Gesellschaft* 12: 1253–68.

Pörzgen, Hermann (1935), "Das deutsche Fronttheater." Cologne: University of Cologne, PhD dissertation.

Prokopovych, Markian (2014), *In the Public Eye: the Budapest Opera House, the Audience and the Press, 1884–1918*. Vienna: Böhlau.

Pschibl, Kerstin (1999), "Das Interaktionssystem des Kabaretts: Versuch einer Soziologie des Kabaretts." Regensburg: University of Regensburg, PhD dissertation.

Pungur, Joseph ed. (2012), *Hungarian World Encyclopedia*. Edmonton, Alberta: Corvin Historical Society.

Segal, Harold B. (1987), *Turn-of-the-Century Cabaret: Paris, Barcelona, Berlin, Munich, Vienna, Cracow, Moscow, St. Petersburg, Zurich*. New York: Columbia University Press.

Seigel, Jerrold (1986), *Bohemian Paris: Culture, Politics, and Boundaries of Bourgeois Life, 1830–1930*. New York: Viking.

Senelick, Laurence (1989), *Cabaret Performance*, Vol. I. New York: PAJ.

Shattuck, Roger (1969), *The Banquet Years*. New York: Vintage.

Shaw, Charles G. (1931), *Nightlife: An Intimate Guide to New York After Dark*. New York: Day.

Shaw, Leroy R. (1989), "Polyphemus among the Phaeacians: Kraus, Wedekind, and Vienna," *Modern Austrian Literature* 22 (3/4): 187–202.

Sonn, Richard D. (1989), *Anarchism and Cultural Politics in Fin de Siècle France*. Lincoln, NE: University of Nebraska Press, 1989.

Sprengel, Peter (1998), *Geschichte der deutschsprachigen Literatur 1870–1900*. Munich: Beck.

Stanislavsky, Konstantin (1987), *Mein Leben in der Kunst*, trans. Klaus Roose. Berlin: Verlag das Europäische Buch.

Stern, Ernst (1951), *My Life, My Stage*. London: Gallancz.

Thompson, Mark Christian (2016), *Kafka's Blues: Figurations of Racial Blackness in the Construction of an Aesthetic*. Evanston, IL: Northwestern University Press.

Traub, Ulrike (2010), *Theater der Nacktheit*. Bielefeld: Transcript.

Trautwein, Elisabeth (2008), Notes to "Biography: Werner Richard Heymann," on the Public Broadcasting Service series *Cinema's*

Exiles: From Hitler to Hollywood, December 2, https://www.pbs. org/wnet/cinemasexilesbiographies/the-composers/biography-werner-richard-heymann/217/

Tucholsky, Kurt (1983a), *Gedichte*. Hamburg: Rowohlt.

Tucholsky, Kurt (1983b), *Briefe. Auswahl 1913–1935*. Berlin: Verlag Volk und Welt.

Türcke, Christoph (1998), "Blasebalg des Unfugs: eine Replik auf Norbert Bolz und sein Lob des Fernsehgeblödels," *Die Zeit,* July 11.

Veigl, Hans (2019), *Fritz Grünbaum und das Wiener Kabarett*. Graz: Österreichisches Kabarettarchiv.

Vogel, Shane (2009), *The Scene of Harlem Cabaret: Race, Sexuality, Performance*. Chicago: University of Chicago Press.

Vossler, Karl (1898), *Das deutsche Madrigal: Geschichte seiner Entwicklung bis in die Mitte des xviii. Jahrhunderts*. Weimar: Felber.

Weinert, Erich (1927), "Besuch bei Max Holz," *Die Weltbühne* 48: 820–2.

Wolzogen, Ernst von (1908), *Ansichten und Aussichten*. Berlin: Fontane.

INDEX